Issue Voting

Ole Borre

Issue Voting

An Introduction

AARHUS UNIVERSITY PRESS

Issue Voting. An Introduction

Copyright: Aarhus University Press 2001
Cover design: Kitte Fennestad
Printed in Denmark at Narayana Press, Gylling
ISBN 87 7288 913 6

Aarhus University Press
Langelandsgade 177
DK-8200 Århus N

Fax: (+45) 89 42 53 80
www.unipress.dk

73 Lime Walk
Headington, Oxford OX3 7AD
United Kingdom

Fax: (+44) 1865 750 079

Box 511
Oakville, CT 06779
USA

Fax: (+1) 860 945 9468

Published with financial support from
The Danish Research Council for the Humanities

Foreword

The original plan of this book was to assess whether there has been a general rise in issue voting. But I abandoned it when I realized that the interest in this hypothesis among scholars in the field has been superseded by an interest in many other ideas related to issue voting. Their ideas should not be reduced and twisted to answer the question of whether issue voting has been rising – a question which they do not address.

Rather, this book is an attempt to provide an outline of the many different models that are used to express issue voting. What is the logic of these models? How are they related to one another? How well do they work? Do they contain pitfalls that one should have in mind when using them? I believe these questions deserve an introductory treatment, considering how many researchers and students are occupied with survey analysis of political attitudes and behavior.

I have followed two guidelines in order to provide a sort of common denominator for the various chapters in the book. One is that I have relied as far as possible on simple statistics, inclining toward linear regression wherever it is possible. The other is that in addition to reviewing the hypotheses I try to illustrate them by means of data from British and Danish general elections. The British data were near at hand when I began working on the book in the spring of 1998 during a stay at Nuffield College in Oxford, and Anthony Heath kindly lent me the fresh 1997 election data. I had just completed a book on the Danish 1994 election with Jørgen Goul Andersen, and the Danish 1998 election was held during my stay at Nuffield. It was plausible to use these elections to provide examples from two different political systems in regard to size, election rules, and the number of parties.

However, the book does not contain a systematic review of the field and the state of our knowledge about issue voting. To undertake such a task in a conscientious manner would prevent me from digging into the many interesting facets of the models. Therefore, only in the last chapter I attempt to look at the broader context in which the models of issue voting can be fitted.

Neither does the book contain systematic hypothesis testing which might bring new knowledge to the field. That is done more properly in articles, and certainly it would require more than illustrative material from

Britain and Denmark. Nonetheless, even illustrating a model with data from a recent election may suggest how well or poorly it works.

I have greatly benefited from criticism, especially by my colleague Jørgen Elklit, of an earlier version of the manuscript. Nevertheless, I am sure that many inconsistencies can still be found in the book. It should be viewed as the product of work in progress and a collection of ideas for the continued study of issue voting.

Finally, I wish to thank Helge and Hedvig Hoff's Foundation for a grant which covered part of the printing expenses of the book.

O.B., March 2001

Contents

Chapter 1. Introduction 9
Early Electoral Research 10
The Rise in Issue Voting 11
What Is Issue Voting? 13
Issues and Cognitive Consistency 14
A Typology of Survey Items on Issues 16

Chapter 2. The Linear Position Model 19
How to Code Consistency 20
A British Example 21
Class Voting and Issue Voting 24
Multiple Issues 28
The Role of Information 30
The Problem of Nonlinearity 32
Accounting for Electoral Change 33
Conclusion 38

Chapter 3. Party Loyalty and Electoral Change 40
Causality and Party Loyalty 41
The Normal Vote Model 43
The European Context 46
A Test on British Data 48
Response Error 50
Party Switching and Controls for Past Vote 53
Types of Election 56
Conclusion 57

Chapter 4. Party Position and Utility 58
The Spatial Approach. 58
The "Nearest Party" Hypothesis 59
Mediated Issue Positions 62
Party Strategy 63
Proximity and Utility 65
Testing the Proximity/Utility model 67
Directional Theory 73

Real and Perceived Party Position 78
Conclusion 82

Chapter 5. Issue Dimensions and Party Systems 83
The Left-Right Schema 84
Left-Right Self-Placement 85
Value Dimensions 88
New Politics 89
Criticism of the New Politics Paradigm 91
Factor Analysis of Issue Dimensions 91
New Politics and the Party System 92
Issue Dimensions in Denmark 93
Issue Dimensions in Britain 95

Chapter 6. Issue Priority 99
Measuring Issue Priority 100
Combining Salience and Position 102
Trading Off Valence Issues 105
The Salience Model 105
Conclusion 109

Chapter 7. Performance and Retrospective Voting 110
Retrospective Voting 110
Performance Evaluations 114
Performance and Electoral Change 117
Combining Salience and Performance: Issue Ownership 119
Economic Voting 122
Sociotropic Voting versus Policy Voting 123
Conclusion 126

Chapter 8. The Causes of Issue Voting 127
Self-Interest or Symbolic Politics? 127
Affect and Cognition 129
The Theory of Cognitive Mobilization 131
New Politics Theory and Issue Voting 132
A Rise in Issue Voting? 134
Linkage Studies 136
The Issue Attention Cycle 140

References 142
Subject Index 156
Author Index 161

Chapter 1

Introduction

In the early days of West European or American democracy, it would not have occurred to any observer to doubt the role of issues in shaping the party systems. Liberal parties were formed with the explicit intention of removing privileges and extending voting rights to new groups, to lift the regulation of business by the state, and to ensure civil rights in speech and printing. In response, conservative parties were formed around issue positions defending the military establishment, the church and the monarchy. Where the lower classes had acquired the right to vote, socialist parties emerged with such issues as the rights of organizing into trade unions, complaints about working conditions or the quality or price of housing, and other social issues. Agrarian parties typically promoted such issues as land distribution and guaranteed prices or import duties on farm products.

Also, during this lively formative period, partisan change at election time was usually explained as the impact of new issues, or the occurrence of events with a high issue-content, such as the Dreyfus affair in France, or the Boer War engaging British politics. Military defeats, public scandals, or a downturn in business visibly affected the support for the governing party. By and large, it was taken for granted that elections were determined by policies and their outcomes – by the parties taking issue positions that were later proved by events to be wise or stupid, fortunate or unfortunate, human or cynical, et cetera. Basically, voting was seen as issue voting.

The idea of issue voting is that of society taking control of its own destiny. According to the logic of issue voting, voters first decide their stands on the policy issues of the day by considering their own interest, their beliefs about what is in the country's interest, moral judgments, or assessment of the records of the government. They then acquire information about the positions and arguments of the competing parties or candidates. Thirdly, they vote for that party or candidate who matches their own stands more accurately, especially on issues that they consider vital. To the extent that the voters, or at least a critical share of them, behave according to that logic, the outcome is an election result and a government that expresses the collective policy stands of the electorate, the "will of the people."

Early Electoral Research

The assessment of how well the public conforms to the ideals of issue voting had to await the development of opinion and attitude measurement,
which meant the development of the theory of mass surveys during and
after the Second World War. Proper sampling and interviewing techniques
according to contemporary standards were not put to use until the Erie
County study of the American presidential election of 1940. The report of
that study, *The People's Choice* (Lazarsfeld, Berelson and Gaudet 1944),
became a landmark in voting research as well as in communications research, cross-breeding the three major fields of psychology, sociology, and
political science.

However, on the topic of issue voting the early election studies was a
disappointment, as there seemed to be little evidence of issue voting. *The
People's Choice* investigated a few issues: for example, Roosevelt's election
for a third term, and participation in the war in Europe. But the authors
doubted very much whether these issues had influenced the voters, apart
from reinforcing party loyalties. The ordinary American voter appeared to
vote out of loyalty to his primary group and according to prevailing norms
in larger secondary groups characterized by their religion or economic
class. The vote was a habit rather than a decision, social rather than political behavior.

Subsequent studies of elections both in the United States and England
seemed to confirm the low amount of issue voting. Researchers from the
University of Michigan had launched a series of nationwide election surveys, expanding the surveys from minor communities to the whole nation,
and from the individual election to consecutive elections. Even so, issue
voting did not gain a place in empirical science that compared with its
standing in democratic theory. The Michigan school favored a psychological rather than a sociological approach and attempted to decompose the
vote into three attitudes: party identification, candidate orientation, and
issue orientation. But judging from their main study, *The American Voter*
(Campbell, Converse, Miller and Stokes 1960), which during the 1960s
became the Bible for students of electoral behavior, party identification
turned out to be the main psychological force, which strongly influenced
candidate and issue orientation. Among the latter, candidate orientation
often appeared stronger than issue orientation in accounting for the
change in the presidential vote from one election to the next.

On the European side of the Atlantic Ocean, the prevailing conclusion
during the 1960s was similar: issue voting was limited to small and well-

informed segments of the electorate, whereas the voters at large mainly voted along lines defined by class, ethnicity, religion, or geographical region. Leading studies such as the anthology *Party Systems and Voter Alignments* (Lipset and Rokkan 1967) and *Political Change in Britain* (Butler and Stokes 1969) contained very little about issues.

During the early phase of voting research, however, two attempts were made to base electoral theory on issues. One was Downs' *An Economic Theory of Democracy* (1957), which applied rational theory to develop hypotheses about voting behavior. Among other things, Downs reasoned in terms of an issue, or policy, space, in which both parties and electors were moving. That approach became important in later research but at the time attracted few customers among the survey analysts. The other was Key's *The Responsible Electorate* (1966), which argued that voters looked retrospectively at the success of governments and rewarded or punished governments for developments under their rule. These developments can of course be specified for different issue areas. But still, retrospective voting is a rudimentary form of issue voting. It entails that whatever policy ideas the voter might have fancied, he should be persuaded by the good results of the government to vote for it even if it chose a different line of policy.

The Rise in Issue Voting

As long as no independent effect of issue orientations on the vote of the mass public could be discerned, the empirical studies naturally concentrated on those social factors that accounted more convincingly for the individual voting choice. This was the situation in the early 1970s, when at last evidence of rising issue voting began to pour in, both in the United States and in European democracies. In the United States, a symposium on issue voting in *American Political Science Review* (Boyd, Brody and Page, Pomper 1972) proposed the hypothesis of a rise in issue voting during the 1960s. Furthermore, an analysis of correlations between issue orientations 1956-72 (Nie with Andersen 1974) sought to revise the picture of inherent limitations in the public's political belief systems, which the Michigan school had painted in an influential article (Converse 1962). In Europe, doubts about the stability of party identification spread (Budge, Crewe and Farlie 1976), and postwar voter generations were seen to carry a new set of values and issues into the political scene (Inglehart 1971).

The rise in issue voting has been welcomed by political commentators as evidence showing that democracy is still sound: rather than an indifferent or alienated mass we find an increasingly enlightened and self-conscious public. But, as is the case with the material and technical development of modern capitalism, there are different interpretations of the trend. The issue voter may not be an informed and engaged participant but a spoilt consumer who demands the impossible from his government and is unwilling to share any responsibility for the political cost and consequences.

Thus, the issue voting hypothesis, which states that present-day voters are strongly influenced by issues and that issues largely determine election outcomes in modern parliamentary systems, is difficult to evaluate both in terms of democratic behavior, in terms of responsible citizen behavior, and in terms of rational self-interested behavior. The literature presents too many diverse approaches to issue voting to permit such an assessment. Empirical studies of single elections nearly always include one or several chapters on the relationship of issues to party preference. But they go about it in ways that often fit an *ad hoc* model to the concrete election and which cannot be compared with other survey studies. Students of multi-party systems, such as the Swedish, Norwegian, or Dutch, produce illustrative maps of the spatial positions of various parties' voters in two issue dimensions. British studies focus on the Conservative vote or the Labour vote, showing how it is affected by various issues. German scholars analyze whether a CDU/CSU government is seen as superior to an SPD government in reaching various policy goals. It is clear that the assessment of issue voting varies according to the method used.

In addition to the election studies, there are professional articles dealing with the theory of issue voting or presenting and testing models of issue voting on a few elections. But in general these articles give rise to discussions in a specific sub-field of issue voting, relatively unconnected with other sub-fields. For example, the large literature on survey evidence of economic voting, which followed upon the Kinder and Kiewiet article in 1979, has been dominated by the discussion between the adherents of "pocketbook" voting and those of "sociotropic" voting. It has not attempted to integrate sociotropic voting into a theory of issue voting so as to compare economic with non economic issues. As another example, the discussion about proximity theory and directional theory which began with the Rabinowitz/Mcdonald article in 1989 has been concerned with showing the advantage of the directional model as a predictor of party sympathy or "utility", but it has not moved on to the act of voting.

What Is Issue Voting?

In presenting and evaluating different models of issue voting, we must first decide what constitutes issue voting, and here we need to be flexible. According to the Oxford Dictionary (1989), an issue is "an important topic for discussion, a point in question, a matter being discussed or debated". Hence it follows that the Prime Minister's private life can also be an issue! Surely we want to limit the term to issues about political goals or policies, that is, to questions about what the government should do and how it should do it.

But even so, issues are a multidimensional concept, its dimensions ranging from those that are employed by the most engaged and informed citizens to those crossing the minds of the indifferent voter. In the first class we place issues about the goals of policies, where they divide the participants into ordered positions on a scale of contrasting views about the end result to be achieved or approached in politics, such as a more egalitarian income distribution. Such voters may also be concerned with the means or policy instruments by which a given goal should be approached, and about the possible side effects of these means. For example, a more egalitarian income distribution may be sought or pursued by means of progressive taxation, extending welfare services, or controlling private business. Lower down on the scale, issues take the form of discussions about what should be on top of the political agenda, that is, questions about priorities. Some voters, though unable to specify any long-term solution to a problem, agree that the problem is more urgent than other problems and requires action by the government. In the same vein, they tend to evaluate the government's performance in the policy area concerned. Finally, debates arise as to whether the situation in a certain policy area should be viewed positively or negatively. At this stage even the politically least involved voter may join the discussion with bits of news stories or personal experiences.

The authors of *The American Voter* (Campbell et al. 1960) realized that the issue content in the vote decision varies in this way, but they set a rather high standard for voting to qualify as issue voting. On each issue that the voter considered important, he should have a preferred policy position. He should be informed about the positions of the parties but choose his position autonomously. He should then compare the distances to different parties and choose the nearest one.

According to these strict requirements, few voters could be called issue voters. Later research, however, has found an abundance of issue-related voting behavior also among voters who fall short of these standards. We need a much broader concept of issue voting to incorporate these findings. Below, I shall draw upon a general social-psychological model to provide such a framework.

Issues and Cognitive Consistency

Issue voting establishes, as a minimal requirement, a three-way relation between a voter, a party, and a political goal or issue, as shown in Figure 1.1.

The voter has an orientation (V) toward the goal. Similarly the party has an orientation (P) toward the same goal. Thirdly, the voter has an attitude (A) toward the party, which manifests itself in a likelihood of voting for it. Each of these orientations may be positive, neutral, or negative.

Various theories of cognitive consistency, congruity, or consonance (Brown 1965) concur in postulating that the voter will be motivated to establish a situation in which the three relationships, or bonds, are positive, and to avoid a situation in which one is negative while the other two are positive. Thus voters with a given goal will tend to like a party that favors the same goal as they do themselves. If one of the three bonds is negative,

Figure 1.1. The Consistency Model of Issue Voting

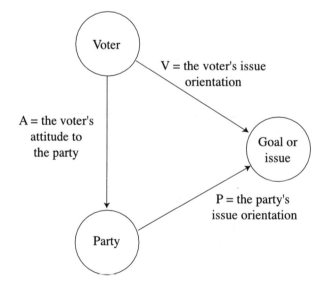

the voter is said to be in a situation of inconsistency, incongruity, or disso-nance, which is supposed to be unpleasant.

An inconsistency can be repaired, of course, by changing the negative bond into a positive one. The voter may (1) change his attitude toward the party from negative to positive on discovering that the party actually has the same goal as he himself. Or he may (2) change his orientation to the goal from negative to positive if he discovers that a party he likes does not share his goal. Finally, if he has a positive orientation to a goal but likes a party that has a negative orientation to the same goal, he (3) will be motiv-ated to distort the party's orientation or refuse to believe that the party has a negative orientation. While case (1) is the standard assumption of ration-al issue voting, case (2) is a way of conforming to the party which is not ir-rational; however, case (3) is generally considered an irrational reaction to the problem of inconsistency.

The point to be taken from the consistency model is that issue voting covers many processes. The finding that there tends to be consistency be-tween V, P, and A does not reveal how this consistency was reached, nor does it reveal what will happen if it is disturbed. Even the three processes mentioned above do not exhaust the possibilities. In addition to them we might mention others that consist in changing a positive bond into a nega-tive one, resulting in one positive and two negative bonds, because such a situation is also believed to be consistent. For example, if a person dislikes a party and discovers that that party has a positive orientation to a goal, this may cause him to acquire a negative opinion of the same goal, simply because he does not want to agree with the party. Or, if he is very commit-ted to his opinion, he may choose instead to refuse to believe that the par-ty really means what it says.

Finally, to extend the analytic possibilities in issue voting, one should realize that concepts like "orientation" and "consistency" apply to several aspects of political issues. A party shows its positive orientation to a goal not only by declaring that in principle it is working toward that goal but also by putting it high on its agenda, and by taking steps toward realizing it when the party is in government. Therefore, issue priority and evalu-ations of issue performance are some of those bonds between parties and issues that we should incorporate in the analysis. In the following chapters we shall often refer back to the model of consistency as a general frame-work in which the hypotheses and findings can be placed.

A Typology of Survey Items on Issues

The evidence of issue voting depends on the availability of interview surveys that measure the respondents' attitudinal and perceptual orientations to a number of political issues. In addition, information is needed about the respondent's party choice and about other attributes and orientations of the respondents that may serve as control variables in the analysis. Mass interview surveys vary a lot in these respects, and in the course of the development of electoral research, surveys in the pioneering countries have developed a great number of measures to tap various aspects of issue voting. The typology given below contains those types of survey items and other (external) data that seem to be the most useful for the analysis of issue voting.

The survey items and related pieces of information have been divided into three main groups. The first set of items, no. 1-3, deal with position issues and concentrate on establishing the relation between the voter's position and the positions of various parties on an issue. These are the types of items that are required for the classical analysis of issue voting, to be discussed in chapters 2-4. However, the mere perception of which party is closest on an issue (type 3) has also been classified in this group, although it is a poor shortcut for the combination of types 1 and 2.

The items in the second set, no. 4-6, are often called salience items. The items in this set mostly concern different societal goals or political values. These are then ordered by the respondent according to their importance. However, salience can also be attached to particular policies on an issue, as when a respondent thinks it is all-important to join the EU, or to keep immigration low. Such policy issues often span several goals – joining the EU, for example, touches both on economic growth, national self-determination, peacekeeping, and possibly other goals too. On the whole, the analytic distinction between goals and policy means will not play a major role in this book, as it seems at odds with political thinking in the mass electorate.

The third group, no. 7-10, here called performance items, concerns the competence or credibility of a government or party in dealing with a particular issue, which need not be a position issue but may be a commonly accepted societal goal such as keeping inflation and unemployment low. Such goals may usually be pursued by different means or policies, thereby giving rise to position issues; but the respondents are not asked to venture their opinions on which policy would be the most proper or efficient in

Table 1.1. Typology of data on issue voting

Position and issue distance items:
1. Respondent's own position on a single issue or an issue scale
    a. Absolute position: Which of these policy alternatives do you prefer?
    b. Relative position: How much do you agree with this policy?
2. Parties' policy positions on an issue or issue scale
    a. External data (party programs and platforms, legislative roll calls, expert judgments, etc.) on the parties' policies
    b. Perceived present/future position of parties: What are the different parties' policies?
    c. Perceived past position: What has been the past government's policy?
    d. Relative position of parties: Which parties will do more (or spend more money), and which will do less (spend less), in a particular policy area?
3. Nearest party: Which party is closest to your position in a particular policy area?

Salience items:
4. How important is a political issue for the respondent (or his/her vote)?
    a. How important is a *particular* political decision on an issue?
5. Relative importance: Which problems or issues are the most important?
6. Agendas: How important is a political problem or issue to the government or party?
    a. External data (party programs and platforms, media data)
    b. Survey data: respondent's perception of the government's or parties' agendas

Performance items:
7. Government handling of a political problem or issue
    a. How well has it handled the problem or issue?
    b. How well will a particular government handle the problem or issue in the future?

8. Comparatively: which party or government best handles a political problem or issue?
    a. Which has handled it best in the past?
    b. Which will handle it best in the future?
9. Did the government or party make the right decision on a particular issue?
    a. Expected future decision: will the government or party make the right decision on a particular issue?
10. Has the development been good or bad in a particular policy area?
    a. Is this the government's desert/fault?
    b. Which future development can be expected?

---

reaching the goal. The distinction between prospective and retrospective orientations, that is, toward the future or the past, plays a large role in sub-dividing the performance items because of the credibility which is at stake: people do not in general vote for parties which they suspect of making un-realistic and empty promises.

The typology offered in Table 1.1 is designed in such a way that it goes from a simple and hard core toward the soft periphery of issue voting. In many respects it is similar to other typologies, such as that of Dalton (1996, 223). Thus there is little disagreement among researchers about the themes of issue voting although, as we shall see, there are different ways of measuring the phenomenon.

Chapter 2
The Linear Position Model

The model of cognitive consistency, which was discussed in Chapter 1, entails that the greater the voter's consistency with the party's issue position, the higher the likelihood of his or her voting for the party, other things equal. The most plausible way of investigating this hypothesis is (1) to break down a sample of respondents by their positions on a certain issue, (2) to argue that these positions differ in the degree of consistency with the party's position, and then (3) to show that the vote for the party increases with increasing consistency. Finally, (4) the condition that other things be equal is met by controlling for other relevant factors that might influence the vote.

Figure 2.1 expresses the relationship between Y, the proportion voting for the party, and X, the voters' issue positions graded in terms of consistency.

Figure 2.1. Linear Model of Issue Voting

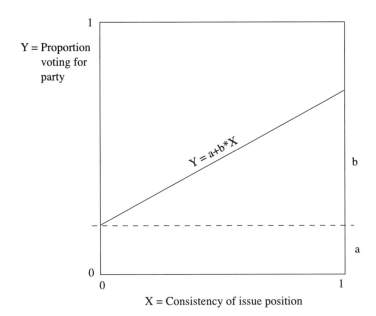

A simple linear relationship, Y=a+b*X with a positive gradient b, is assumed. That is, among voters with issue positions that are completely inconsistent with the party line, we assume that the proportion voting for the party is small (Y=a). It might be argued that none of these inconsistent voters should vote for the party; however, some of these voters might be consistent with the party on other issues, or for various other reasons, which we have not controlled.

We assume that issue consistency (X) can be measured on a scale from 0 to 1. Hence, among voters whose issue positions are perfectly consistent with the party line, we expect the vote for the party to be Y=a+b. We cannot assume that all consistent voters choose the party, so that a+b=1, because these voters may also be consistent with the issue position of another party. Hypothetically, the magnitude of b will depend on both the weight of the issue compared with other factors that the issue is associated with, as well as the competition for issue positions among the parties.

It should be noted that these assumptions do not include a postulate that the causality runs from the issue position to the vote, rather than the reverse. Ordinarily we shall present the data in the form of statistical tables in which the voter's issue position is the independent variable and the vote for the party, the dependent variable. But it follows from the consistency model that the attitude to the party, which is expressed in the vote, may have caused the voter to choose a consistent issue position. This complication will be discussed in the next chapter. In the present chapter we first look at the simple linear relationship between issue positions and partisan strength. Subsequently we discuss how this model can be extended in three directions: (1) by controlling for social position, (2) by adding other issues to the model, and (3) by extending it to two or more elections.

How to Code Consistency

The hypothesis states that the vote is a function of consistency between voter position and party position, between V and P. Obviously, a basic problem in testing the hypothesis is to determine which degree of consistency to attach to different issue positions. There are two leading schools here, proximity theory and directional theory, which we shall discuss further in Chapter 3. While proximity theory looks at issue positions in the spatial sense, directional theory sees them as intentions that generate emotion or "affect". Here we shall follow the path of spatial thinking.

Policy goals may be imagined as positions scattered along a line. In the simplest case the party may have announced an unambiguous stand on the issue. For example, if the party is in favour of Denmark's membership of the European Union, the survey question,

> 'Are you for or against Denmark's membership of the European Common Market?'

gives rise to a coding procedure in which Yes=1, No=0, while Don't Know responses are either discarded or given an in-between value of 0.5. Alternatively these three positions may be coded 2, 0, and 1, or they may be coded +1, -1, and 0. There is no fixed practice, but in case the Don't Knows are coded, the implicit assumption is that these positions are equidistant. This assumption may not be correct because we cannot know in advance whether the Don't Knows are more similar to the adherents than to the opponents.

However, the same issue may call for three, four or even five policy alternatives, all demanding a response category:

> 'Do you think Britain's long-term policy should be to (1) leave the European Community, (2) to stay in the EC and try to reduce its powers, (3) to leave things as they are, (4) to stay in the EC and try to increase its powers, or (5) to work for the formation of a single European government?' (British Election Survey 1992, question 29a)

Even assuming that one of these stands reflects accurately that of the party, are the other stands equidistant? The easiest answer is to look for a way of coding the responses that will make the vote for the party an approximately linear function of the degree of consistency. A statistically more sophisticated answer is to turn to log linear models in which each response category can be looked at as a variable rather as a predetermined code.

The inclination of most researchers is to assume equidistant positions, since this leads to the well-trodden path of linear regression models. The problem of nonlinearity is then pushed into the background till the moment when the linear model fails to work.

A British Example

Fortunately, many relationships are linear or nearly so. Table 2.1 shows a breakdown of the 1992 vote for the three major British parties by the respondents' responses to the item, "Income and wealth should be redistributed towards ordinary working people" (question 47a).

Table 2.1. Vote distribution by position on the income redistribution
issue, in percent (Britain, 1992)

	Cons.	Labour	Lib.Dem.	(N)
1. Strongly agree	13%	65%	12%	(346)
2. Agree	27	46	17	(1136)
3. Not sure either way	47	30	17	(574)
4. Disagree	68	12	16	(720)
5. Strongly disagree	84	6	7	(141)
All respondents who voted	42%	35%	15%	(2917)

The Conservative vote declines from 84 to 13 percent, and the Labour vote
rises from 6 to 65 percent, with the degree of support for income redistribution. The Liberal Democratic vote varies in a curvilinear way from 12 to
17 and back to 7 percent with degree of support.

In the case of the two largest parties, most people would not find it difficult to attach consistency scores to these five response categories. Since
the survey item cites a political goal identified with the Labour Party, it is
clear that the more the voter agrees with that goal, the more likely he or she
will vote for Labour. So, for the Labour vote we should code the consistency
variable from strongly agree=1 to strongly disagree=0. The Conservative
Party is opposed to the same goal, and therefore we should code consistency from strongly disagree=1 to strongly agree=0.

The Liberal Democratic Party does not have a clear stand on the issue
of income redistribution, and hence it follows that the voter's attitude
should have little effect on his or her propensity to vote for that party. Here
we shall assume, however, that position 3, the undecided position, is partly consistent with the position of the Liberal Democratic Party. Therefore
we code this position=0.5, while coding positions 2 and 4=0.25 and positions 1 and 5=0 in the model for the Liberal Democratic vote.

The fact that the two large parties have opposite stands makes the degrees of consistency with these parties complementary to one another. The
more consistent a voter is with the Conservatives, the less consistent the
same voter is with Labour's stand, and vice versa. Hence, the consistency
model is reinforced by the fact that attraction to one party is equal to repul-
sion for the other. No doubt this has added to the strength of the relationship that we find. However, it also means that we cannot test two indepen-

dent hypotheses, one for the Conservative Party and the other for Labour. This will not be possible until we review the utility theory in Chapter 4.

We may now estimate the parameters of regression equations of the form

Vote = a + b * Issue consistency,

where Vote stands for the cell frequencies in one of the columns of Table 2.1, while Issue consistency stands for the recoded row number, and a and b are constant parameters. The estimated equations for the three parties are:

Conservative vote = .10 + .76 No redistribution	(with r=0.45)
Labour vote = – .02 + .65 Redistribution	(with r=0.38)
Liberal Democratic vote = .12 + .12 Undecided	(with r=0.05)

According to these estimates the issue effect is somewhat stronger for the Conservative vote than for the Labour vote, b=0.76 as against b=0.65. The third equation indicates a weak but still positive and significant effect of consistency on the Liberal Democratic vote.

As shown on the right, also the correlation coefficient is higher for the Conservative vote, r= 0.45 for the Conservative vote against r=0.38 for the Labour vote. However, correlation coefficients for relationships in which one of the variables is dichotomous (1 or 0) are unreliable measures of the success of the model in accounting for the vote. Therefore, many other correlation measures are often used in statistical tables. Below, we shall devise a general measure of the level of issue/vote consistency across the three parties on the basis of Table 2.1. If we attach the positions 5, 1 and 3, respectively, to the three parties, the table may be converted to one showing the level of consistency for all voters in the sample (except those voting for minor parties). This is done in Table 2.2.

Table 2.2. Vote distribution by position on the income redistribution issue, in no. of respondents (Britain, 1992)

	1. Labour	3. Lib.Dem.	5. Cons.
1. Strongly agree	225	42	45
2. Agree	523	193	307
3. Not sure either way	172	98	270
4. Disagree	86	115	490
5. Strongly disagree	8	10	114

The table now shows the relationship between voter position and party position, between V and P, for all voters of the three parties in the sample. Therefore, on the basis of the raw number of voters in each cell of the table we may compute the VP correlation, which in this case yields r=0.48. This coefficient expresses the degree of issue voting on the issue of income redistribution.

The substantive interpretation of these coefficients is that we find a comparatively high level of issue voting on the issue of income redistribution for the 1992 election. Apparently, old-style ideologies are still very much alive in British voting behavior. The 1970s have been described as a "decade of dealignment" (Särlvik and Crewe 1983). However, this does not imply that Conservative and Labour voters have moved so close to one another on left-right ideological issues that issue voting has ceased to leave its traces on electoral behaviour during the 1990s.

Class Voting and Issue Voting

The model in Tables 2.1 and 2.2 indicates a level of issue voting but reveals nothing about the underlying causal process. For example, it is plausible to hypothesize that the respondent's social class, income, age, sex, or place of residence influences both the issue position and the vote. Considering the traditional importance of social class position in British voting behavior, it seems especially likely that the respondents' class positions influence both their choice of party and at the same time their positions on ideological issues. Those who disagree with the proposal of redistributing incomes in Table 2.1 or 2.2 are expected to be mainly middle-class voters who vote Conservative anyway. Thus the only requirement they may fulfill is that they report an issue orientation; they may be ignorant of the position taken by the Conservative party, and they may properly claim that their issue position has nothing to do with their preference for that party.

All the same, research on issue voting is often carried out without social position controls. However, the matter is not as simple as that: the analyst may be interested in knowing that the voters do have a sense of issue positions. This was actually the main point that was disputed in the American literature around 1970. Table 2.1 obviously shows that the voters do not make random answers to survey items on issues. If, for example, half of the respondents within each party chose at random among the five response categories, the pattern in the table could never be so distinct, and the distribution in the last column would be more balanced.

In controlling for social class and other background variables, we also remove one part of the vote that is relatively constant from one election to the next. *Changes* in the vote between elections cannot have been caused by these control variables.

In analyzing those European election surveys that have carefully explored the respondents' positions on a number of issues, it seems difficult to find cases in which issue effects vanish after social position controls have been inserted. This is true even for elections of the 1960s and 1970s. For the British 1975 election, Table 2.3 shows the Conservative vote subdivided by both issue position and class position. The issue position was the response to the item, "what is your view about redistributing income and wealth in favour of ordinary working people?" It was coded 1=very important that it should be done, 2=fairly important that it should be done, 3=does not matter, 4=fairly important that it should not be done, and 5=very important that it should not be done. This is an earlier version of the item used in Table 2.1.

If we compare the bottom line of this table with the left-hand row of Table 2.1, we find that the Conservative vote has increased a little in the four first cells and quite a lot in the last – from 70 to 84 percent – over these years. Insofar as we can compare the two slightly different items, the difference between the two extreme issue groups is 58 percent, or somewhat less than the 71 percent found in Table 2.1. This is consistent with the notion

Table 2.3. Conservative vote, by class identification and attitude to income redistribution (British 1975 election)

Class identification	Attitude to income redistribution				
	Positive				Negative
Working class	5%	13%	29%	43%	54%
	(160)	(153)	(63)	(46)	(24)
Middle class	11%	38%	44%	66%	84%
	(47)	(84)	(36)	(73)	(47)
Other or no class	17%	28%	47%	72%	68%
	(212)	(329)	(163)	(212)	(114)
All	12%	25%	42%	67%	70%
	(419)	(566)	(262)	(331)	(185)

that some measure of dealignment took place during 1970s. We find, furthermore, by looking at the Ns in parentheses that public opinion has shifted somewhat toward the right. Both of these changes contributed to increasing the total Conservative vote, which went up from 37 percent in 1975 to 42 percent in 1992 in the samples.

The difference between the rows in Table 2.3 indicates the net effect of social class identification. This effect ranges from a mere 6 percent in the first column to 30 percent in the last. The difference between the five columns indicates the effect of issue orientation. This effect is 49 percent in the working class and 73 percent in the middle class.

The linear regression model is estimated as follows:

Conservative vote = .61 No redistribution + .16 No working class id + .03 Middle class id + .00

Here the variable "No redistribution" was coded from 0 in the left-hand column to 1 in the right-hand column. "No working class id" and "Middle class id" were dummy variables coded 1 or 0. Therefore, when both are 1 the respondent has a middle class identification, whereas when only the former is 1 the respondent has no class identification. The coefficients therefore show an issue effect of 0.61, plus a Conservative vote that is 19 and 16 percent higher, for those with middle class and no class identification, respectively, than among those with working class identification.

The controlled issue effect, b=.61, is not much lower than the uncontrolled effect, b=.66. Hence we may conclude that the social class controls do very little to reduce the issue effect. However, it is often pointed out that the comparisons between class effects and issue effects are not quite fair because class position is an antecedent variable to issue position. Therefore, social class position also affects the vote indirectly via its effect on the issue orientation. This might be called the combined effect of class and issue. In Figure 2.2 this is indicated by the two arrows leading from the issue position to the vote. The indirect, or combined, effect is the product of the efect of class position on issue position and the effect of issue position on the vote. The direct issue effect is the remaining effect of issue position on the vote.

In the case of the issue effects we have studied in Table 2.3, the indirect effect of social class may be gauged from a comparison of the direct class effect with the total class effect, which is found by leaving out the issue

Figure 2.2. Class effect, issue effect and combined effect

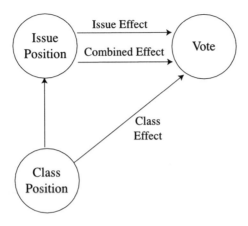

orientation from the regression equation. This results in the regression equation:

Conservative vote = .25 No working class id + .07 Middle class id

If we compare this equation with the foregoing, we find that the effect of No working class has declined by .09, and the effect of Middle class identification, by .04, by the addition of the issue to the equation. These are therefore combined effects, which might be deducted from the issue effect of .61. Even so, there remain issue effects that are about twice as strong as the class effects.

These figures suggest that although class voting is certainly not negligible in modern British elections, issue voting is a far stronger force. At least in 1975, many believed that the British electorate was still divided along class lines rather than on issues. Therefore it is surprising to find that the issue effect is little affected by the inclusion of social class identification controls. Even though class is of course a background variable influencing both issue orientations and the vote, issue effects are certainly much more than reflections of membership in social class or similar groupings.

The strategy of extending the model with control variables, rather than subdividing the sample, should be preferred because it keeps up a large number of respondents in the analysis. However, it implies an assumption that the issue effect is the same in all classes of the control variable. This may not be true: for example, according to Table 2.3 it is the middle-class vote that appears to be particularly affected by the issue position. Thus we may venture the hypothesis that a steady trend toward a weakening of the working class and a strengthening of the middle class will induce a higher amount of issue voting in Britain. This is slightly different from the more common view that that the long-term decline of traditional class voting leads to an increase in issue voting (Franklin 1985a, 1985b). If this were true, we would expect those without class identification to exhibit a higher level of issue voting than those with either working class or middle class identification.

Multiple Issues

Among the most obvious advantages of the linear model is that it easily extends from one to two or more issues. It seems particularly important to control the issue voting models for the impact of other issues than the one we are presently concerned with. In parallel with the rise in issue voting there may be expected a closer correlation between different issues. The lesson has been that nowadays, no issue can be studied in isolation from other issues. The development of issue clusters will be discussed further in Chapter 5. At present we are merely concerned with the question of how the issue voting model may be generalized to two or more dimensions.

In their study of the British 1983 election the authors of *How Britain Votes* (Heath, Jowell and Curtice 1985) present a table (p. 119) indicating the dependency of the vote of the three major competing parties on the voter's position on two issues, nuclear armament and the nationalization of private business. In Table 2.4 only the Conservative vote is shown.

According to the table, the Conservative vote varies substantially with the respondent's position on both issues, so that the combined variation runs from 9% in the upper left corner to 77% in the lower right one. We want to know to what extent the consistency model of issue voting explains the Conservative vote. However that model can be formulated in several versions from the table: consistency in respect to the nationalization issue, with respect to the nuclear arms issue, or with respect to both issues at the same time.

The linear model can be varied to answer these questions. By inserting first one, then the other, and finally both issues in the model, it will pro-

Table 2.4. Percent voting Conservative, by position on two issues

	Nationalize private companies	No change	Sell off nationalized companies
Reduce nuclear weapons	9% (315)	11% (326)	41% (345)
No change	16% (109)	30% (338)	72% (547)
Increase nuclear weapons	32% (129)	52% (177)	77% (695)

Source: Heath, Jowell and Curtice (1985), p.119. No. of respondents (=100%) in parentheses.

vide uncontrolled and controlled effects of the two issues on the vote. The Conservative Party is assumed to be in favor of selling off nationalized companies and to increase nuclear weapons. Therefore, consistency runs from 0 to 1 both downward and toward the right in the table. The result of the regression analysis is the following equation.

Conservative vote = .46 Privatization + .33 Nuclear armament – .02 (R=0.51)

The two coefficients indicate the estimated change in the vote resulting from a change in issue position from left to right, respectively from top to bottom, in the table. The effect is slightly larger for the nationalization issue than for the nuclear weapons issue.

The issue effect of privatization is markedly lower here than in the un-controlled model or the model with social class identification controls. This suggests that it is not meaningful to speak of issue effects unless they are controlled for other issues. When the issue space is conceived to have two dimensions, as in this case, or even more dimensions, these dimensions may of course not be equally important in explaining the variations in the vote. Our results suggest that the nationalization issue is more important than the nuclear armament issue. The number of issues incorporated in the model can of course be extended to three or more, according to how many issues influence the vote in a given election. However, if these issues are closely related to each other, there appears a problem of collinearity, in which the arbitrary choice of one issue tends to reduce the effect of the others because the vote depends on the combined effect of these issues.

This calamity can be avoided by combining the issues into an additive index. In Table 2.4 such an index would range from a consistency value of 0 in the upper left cell to 1 in the lower right cell, counting every step as 0.25 either toward the right or downward. In this case it turns out that the correlation between such an index and the Conservative vote is also 0.51. That is, simplifying the model by jumbling the two issues has not reduced its predictive power.

Indeed, such a simple model is merely a reformulation of the one used by British researchers to classify voters according to whether these voters are pro-Labour or pro-Conservative on a set of issues (Dunleavy and Husbands 1985). In Table 2.4, obviously those in the upper left corner are pro-Labour on both issues, while those in the lower right corner are pro-Conservative on both issues. So, from the upper left to the lower right corner the Conservative/Labour balance shifts from -2 to +2.

Combining several issues into an index eliminates the risk of collinearity. It also reduces the problem of reliability, or the tendency of respondents to give random answers. On the other hand, one should be aware of the risk that the separate effects of one or two dominant issues is overlooked, when they are polluted by the presence of other issues in the same index.

The Role of Information

The effect of issue orientations upon the vote must be assumed to vary with the voter's level of political information. This follows from the consistency model we introduced in Chapter 1. Unless the voter knows the party's position on the issue, he does not know how much his own position agrees or disagrees with it. Therefore he cannot attain consistency between his issue orientation and his vote, except by sheer luck or by distorting the party's position so that it coincides with his own.

The relevant knowledge is, of course, the party's position on the particular issue in which we are interested. But this may be assumed to have a strong general component, so that voters with high political interest or a high level of education are expected to be better than other voters in assessing the positions of different parties on different issues.

For Table 2.5 we divided the voters in the British 1997 election survey according to their school leaving age: below 16, 16-18, and above 18 years

Table 2.5. Percent voting Conservative 1997, by school leaving age and opinion on taxes and social benefits

School Leaving Age	Keep or Reduce Taxes and Benefits	Increase Taxes and Benefits	Difference in Conservative Voting
Below 16 Years	47 (204)	20 (584)	27
16-18 Years	53 (249)	26 (587)	27
Above 18 Years	69 (86)	15 (276)	54
All	53 (539)	21 (1447)	32

of age. We also divided them according to whether they thought the government should increase taxes and spend more on health, education, and social benefits, or whether it should keep these activities at the same level or a reduced level. The two latter options were combined, as only few wanted to reduce the activities. For each of the cells, Table 2.5 shows the percent voting Conservative.

We find that on both issue positions, those who left school at 16-18 years are slightly more Conservative than those who left school earlier, but the difference between the issue positions is the same, 27 percentage points. However, those who left school after their 18th year are more Conservative if they agree with the Conservative stand, and less Conservative if they disagree with it. The difference between these issue positions is twice as high, or 54 percent.

Somewhat similar differences are found if other indicators than school leaving age are used for the voter's level of political information. The issue effect typically is greater for those with a high level of information than for those with a lower level. We may express this rather simply by letting the regression coefficient vary with the level of information. If we use standardized variables that are transformed to have a mean of 0 and a standard deviation of 1, we may estimate the interaction effect from the regression function

Vote = b Issue position + c Issue position * Information level.

For example, if the voter's self-assessed political interest, coded in five steps from 5=a great deal of interest to 1=not at all interested, is used to signify the political information level, we estimate the following function:

Conservative vote = .24 Issue position + .09 Issue position * Political interest.

This implies that the issue effect is estimated to be 0.24 for the average voter, but 0.33 for those with a political interest one standard deviation above the average level, and only 0.15 for those with an interest one standard deviation lower than the average. Both coefficients are strongly significant.

The Problem of Nonlinearity

In many cases the relationship between the vote and an issue orientation is monotonous – rising or falling across the whole issue scale – but nonlinear. This is especially the case when the proportions voting for a particular party in at least some issue positions are either very low, 10 percent or more, or very high, above 90 percent. Examining the 1994 and 1998 elections in Denmark, the example below (Table 2.6) illustrates the dependency of the rightwing vote on the refugee issue. The vote for the right-wing parties (Progressive Party in 1994, Progressive Party and Danish People's Party in 1998) was 16.6 percent in 1994 and 28.1 in 1998 among those who thought that far too many refugees are allowed into Denmark. From this maximum value it dropped first rapidly, then more gently, toward zero among respondents with less restrictive attitudes.

The ordinary linear model is not capable of expressing such a dramatically J-shaped relationship. Instead, it has become standard practice to apply

Table 2.6. Relation between the support for rightwing parties in Denmark in the1994 and 1998 elections and attitudes toward refugees.

	Rightwing 1994	Vote 1998	Log Odds 1994 1998	Level of Consistency Linear Squared Cubic		
Denmark should receive:						
Far fewer	16.6% (356)	28.1 (423)	-1.61 -0.94	1	1	1
Fewer	4.4 (498)	6.0 (608)	-3.07 -2.66	.75	.56	42
As now	1.6 (590)	2.4 (559)	-4.12 -3.89	.50	.25	13
More	0.1 (195)	0.1 (160)	-6.91 -6.91	.25	.06	02
Far more	0.0 (30)	0.0 (44)	-7.50 -7.50	0	0	0

Note. Numbers in parentheses indicate Ns (=100 percent).

logistic regression, which has the property of yielding vote estimates within the logical interval between 0 and 100 percent. By converting the dependent variable Y from percentages to the natural logarithm of the odds for voting for the party, log Y/(1-Y), one constructs a variable, the logit, which has no upper or lower limit. When the vote is 99%, the logit becomes 4.60. When the vote is 90% the logit is 2.20. At 50% the logit will be 0. At 10% the logit will be close to -2.20. And when the vote is 1% the logit will be -4.60. Thus instead of a variable running from 0.01 to 0.99 we get a variable running between -4.6 and +4.6 with particularly high precision at both ends. In the interval between 20 and 80 percent the effects in a log odds model are approximately four times larger than the corresponding effects in a linear model. In the interval below 20 or above 80 percent the effects in the log odds model quickly become much larger. If logarithms with base 10 are used instead of logarithms with base e, the log odds are 2.3 times lower.

The logit data in the middle columns are approximately linear. A minor problem is that for the two last observations an artificial low value (here, -7.5) must be inserted, as the logarithm of zero is not defined. A regression line may be computed for the series of observations, and if one desires, the estimated vote for the five points on the issue scale may be calculated in terms of percent voting rightwing, and compared with the actual percentages in the table.

The logistic regression model has some advantages over the linear model, but one might also consider regression functions that manipulate the independent rather than the dependent variable. For example, if we hypothesize that extremist and single-issue parties tend to rely on voters who agree completely, not just partially, with the party line, we might experiment with a measure of consistency that is a quadratic or higher-order function of the issue scale. The right-hand part of the table shows the linear, square, and cubic forms of the issue scale. It turns out that especially the cubic form correlates with the voting probabilities in Table 2.6 both for 1994 and 1998.

Thus, an alternative to logistic regression is to translate issue positions into consistency according to some nonlinear function.

Accounting for Electoral Change

The models we have studied so far are static in the sense that each of them contains data from one election at a time. The coefficients of such models tell us nothing about the underlying causal relationships. The voters' issue positions may have caused their choice of party, or their choice of party may have caused their issue positions, or both may have been caused by some third factor. This is true even if we control for other factors: within each control group, the causality may run in both directions.

This means that we cannot expect the coefficients of these models to tell us what will happen if the voters change their issue positions or their party choices from one election to the next. If public opinion changes by one unit toward the Conservative pole on the redistribution issue in Britain, will the Conservative vote increase by 19 percent, as it should according to the data in Table 2.1? We cannot tell from one election only because we do not know how the parties will react to such a momentous opinion change. It is likely that the other parties will anticipate a loss and change their positions on the redistribution issue in the direction of public opinion. However, by conducting the analysis for two or more elections, we may dissect the election outcome into various components. If we look at the simple linear model,

Vote = a + b * Issue consistency,

we see that the aggregated vote for the party will rise either

(1)   if the constant a rises;
(2)   if the constant b rises, or
(3)   if the aggregated issue consistency rises.

Obviously, Case (1) constitutes an across-the-board increase in the strength of the party and therefore may be unrelated to the issue. Case (2) constitutes a rise in issue voting such that the party gains more votes on its home ground, that is, at or near its own issue position. In case (3) the party gains because public opinion turns to the party's favour so that proportionally more voters rally to the party's position.

In order to study these possibilities, let us compare the British 1992 and 1997 elections with a view to decompose the Labour victory.

Table 2.7 shows the percent voting Labour in 1992 and 1997 by the voters' attitude to income redistribution. Within each issue position there was a substantial increase in the Labour vote, between 13 and 8 percentage points. However, the degree of issue voting was the same in both elections. This is seen from the regression lines for the two elections:

1992:   Labour vote = – .01 + .64 Redistribution   (r= .38)
1997:   Labour vote = .10 + .64 Redistribution   (r= .37).

Table 2.7. Labour vote 1992 and 1997, by attitude to income redistribution.

Issue orientation	Voted Labour 1992	Voted Labour 1997	Change 1992-97
1. Strongly agree	65 (346)	77 (385)	+12
2. Agree	46 (1136)	56 (795)	+10
3. Not sure	30 (574)	42 (363)	+12
4. Disagree	12 (720)	25 (358)	+13
5. Strongly disagree	6 (141)	14 (97)	+8
Whole sample	35 (2917)	50 (1998)	+15

Note. No. of respondents in parentheses.

In both elections the Labour vote is estimated to vary on average by 16 percent of the vote for rows in the table, or by 64 percent from top to bottom. The difference between the two elections appears in the constant parameter, a, which has grown from – .01 to + .10. This means that in each issue position the Labour Party got 11 percent more votes in the last election than in the first. This increase in the Labour vote occurred across the five issue positions and is therefore independent of the redistribution issue. It takes the form of an upward shift of the 1992 line.

But as seen in the last row of Table 2.7, the Labour vote increased from 35 to 50 percent in the aggregate. How do we account for the remaining 4 percent increase? The answer is found in the distribution of opinions, shown in parentheses. The average issue position changed from 2.72 in 1992 to 2.49 in 1997, that is, toward the left according to traditional notions of left and right. This opinion change favoured the Labour Party by the remaining 4 percent. This component takes the form of a change along the regression line rather than an upward shift in that line.

Looking at the two regression equations, we should realize that they could be compressed into one. If the 1997 election is represented as a dummy variable, Election 97, the general equation can be written

Labour vote = – .01 + .11 Election 97 + .64 Redistribution.

If, however, the coefficient of Redistribution had changed from 1992 to 1997, it would have been necessary to complicate the regression equation further by incorporating an interaction term in the form of the product of Redistribution and Election 97. The coefficient of this product would register how much the issue effect of the 1997 election deviated from the .64 in the 1992 election.

Another example is the recovery of the British Conservative Party in 1979 after its decline in the 1974 elections. Table 2.8 relates the party's vote to the public's issue position on the nationalization versus privatization issue.

These percentages indicate a rise in Conservative support from 7 to 14 percent among "nationalizers" and from 67 to 74 percent among "privatisers", partly offset by a decline from 48 to 38 percent among "neutrals". However, the Ns in parentheses reveal that a strong change in the opinion climate took place from nationalization to privatization. If the percentages had been the same in 1979 as they were in 1974, we may compute that the change in opinion climate alone would cause a rise in the Conservative vote in the sample from 39 to over 49 percent. If the Ns had remained in 1979 what they were in 1974, but the percentages had changed as above, the Conservative vote would have declined to 38 percent.

Thus, the entire gain for the Conservative Party is explainable by a decrease in aggregate public support for nationalization. This is also revealed by the regression equations corresponding to the above figures:

1974:   Conservative vote = .10 + .64 Privatization   (with r=0.47)
1979:   Conservative vote = .09 + .64 Privatization   (with r=0.45),

where the Conservative vote is coded 1 or 0, while the attitude is coded 1=more privatization, 0.5=stay the same, and 0=more nationalization. We see that the same equation appears in both elections. Consequently the surge of the Conservative vote, which according to the sample went up from 37 percent in October 1974 to 48 percent in 1979, may be accounted for solely by the right shift in the electorate, away from nationalization and

Table 2.8. Conservative vote October 1974 and 1979, by attitude to nationalization.

	More nationalization	Stay the same	More privatization
1974	7% (547)	48% (795)	67% (363)
1979	14% (224)	38% (624)	74% (594)

toward privatization. The mean position on the issue shifted dramatically toward the right from 0.45 in October 1974 to 0.62 in 1979, making for a much greater average consistency of voters with the Conservative position. This shift is also visible in the numbers in parentheses. The shift of 0.17 points, when multiplied by the issue effect of 0.64, exactly accounts for the eleven percent increase in Mrs. Thatcher's first election.

In this case it is proper to apply the effect model uncontrolled for class or party identification or other predispositions. This is because the two elections are so close to one another in time that it can be assumed that changes in these predispositions are small compared with the magnitude of the electoral shift.

However, naturally other issue models might have explained the October 1974-1979 change just as well. The Thatcher triumph has for example been ascribed to demands for lower taxes and government spending (Pettersen 1995, 123), or to a rightward turn in several attitudes (Norris 1997, 164-71). Thus it would of course be necessary to control for other pertinent issues on which public opinion may have changed between the two elections.

If a nonlinear model of the vote for a party is applied to two or more elections, a similar decomposition of the electoral change is possible. From looking at the vote for the radical right in Denmark (Table 2.6), we get the impression that the same type of relationship between the vote and the xenophobic attitude to refugees holds for 1994 and 1998. The difference is that at each issue position, the right wing was proportionally stronger in 1998 than it was in 1994. This also becomes expressed in the log odds model, which is:

1994: Log odds Rightwing = -6.86 + 5.19 Xenophobia   (r= .31)
1998: Log odds Rightwing = -6.86 + 5.75 Xenophobia   (r= .33)

What made the difference between the two elections is that the coefficient of the xenophobic attitude rose from 5.19 in 1994 to 5.75 in 1998. Presumably this was the result of an increased salience of the refugee issue in 1998. Compared with this factor, the change in the opinion distribution was negligible.

We have seen here examples of two ideal types of issue voting. One ideal type is characterized by public opinion on the issue turning toward left or right, causing a shift in the vote as predicted by the regression line. This is exemplified by the Conservative surge in Britain at the 1979 election, which we interpret as caused by a rightward shift in attitudes related to income redistribution, nationalization of industry, and similar classical left-right attitudes.

The other ideal type is characterized by the increased salience of an issue, causing a surge for the party that represents a particular issue position. This is exemplified by the Danish rightwing parties in the 1998 election. The increase in the vote for these parties was limited to voters with anti-refugee attitudes. No significant opinion change took place, but probably because the refugee issue became prominent in the period between 1994 and 1998, the effect of these attitudes on the vote increased relative to the previous election.

These two pure types can be distinguished simply by comparing the issue/vote relations for two or more elections. Such a comparison also serves to pinpoint cases that are characterized by a permanent state of issue voting, or what may be called ideological voting. In these cases the vote division appears to be related to a conflict between issue groups, but since the lines of conflict tend to be "frozen", they do not cause electoral change, at least in the short run. Instead, party fortunes shift upward or downward as a result of forces operating across all issue positions.

It should be noted, however, that the analytic separation of these cases presupposes that the competing parties maintain their positions as representatives of particular issue positions over the elections involved in the comparison. The parties are not supposed to move from one position to another. Later, we shall discuss the complications arising when we drop this premise.

Conclusion

In this chapter we have illustrated the strong relationship between issue positions and voting for British and Danish parties. People tend indeed to vote for parties that are in agreement with their opinions on political issues. This is quite in accordance with the model of consistency that was introduced at the end of Chapter 1. In most cases this tendency to issue voting can be demonstrated by means of simple linear models, although the linear model makes a number of assumptions that, when used by researchers, are not always made explicit. Indeed, some of these assumptions are clearly wrong, as any statistician can prove. However, in defence of the model one should appreciate its qualities as a heuristic tool for expressing the basic ideas behind issue voting. Above all, the consistency hypothesis is shown beyond reasonable doubt to hold true, indicating that issue voting is a reality in electoral behaviour. In the next chapter, however, we shall see that the causal process leading to issue voting is much less clear.

Chapter 3
Party Loyalty and Electoral Change

The models we discussed in Chapter 2 treat the vote probability as a function of the voter's issue position (with or without control for other variables). Thereby they mirror the classical view of issue voting, according to which the voter first takes a stand on those issues that he or she considers important, and then looks around for a party that represents these issue positions. Thus the issue voter is assigned a high degree of autonomy.

However, we have anticipated from our consistency model in figure 1.2 that this is only one way of attaining consistency between issue position and party choice. Another way is for the voter to change his or her issue positions so as to accord with the stand of the preferred party. How can this type of causality be incorporated in models of issue voting?

Opinion changes cannot be distinguished from party changes except in panel studies, in which the same respondents are interviewed several times. The cross-sectional design does not permit us to tell these types apart. In studying two successive cross-section surveys, for example from two elections, we can isolate similar groups and note how many have changed party. But we can never tell exactly *who* have changed. It is always possible for voters within a given control group (such as social class) to decide on a party and afterwards adjust their opinions to produce the same pattern as if the decision process had operated the other way round.

It may be added that even panels are of no help in revealing the causality for those panel respondents who turn out to have shifted both their vote and their opinion since the last round of interviewing, which may be the previous election. This would call for multi-wave panels in which the same respondents are interviewed over and over – a procedure that causes attrition of the participants. Panel analysis is a necessary but not a sufficient method for establishing the dynamics operating at the micro level.

Actually, in reality this dynamics turned out to differ markedly from the assumptions of the simple model of issue voting. In the first place, panel analysis disclosed that the independent variable, the issue position, is measured with a large amount of error or unreliability. Thus, if a voter changes his issue position we often suspect that this is not a real change but an element of randomness in answering questions about political opinions. This unreliability was accentuated in an article about "the nature of belief systems in mass public" by the Michigan researcher Philip Converse (1964).

Second, panel analysis in which one of the variables has lagged relative to the other has disclosed that the causality runs in both directions, not only from opinion to party choice but also from party choice to opinion. Indeed, one of the earliest findings was that by far the largest proportion changed their opinion in the direction of their party, rather than the reverse. In the study of the 1940 election it was found that vote intention earlier in the campaign caused changes in opinion (about whether a president could be elected for a third term in office) much more frequently than the opinion caused a change of party preference. This meant that consistency was more often attained by opinion change than by partisan change (Lazarsfeld, Berelson and Gaudet 1968, xi).

Causality and Party Loyalty

Such findings cannot be explained without understanding two notions that were introduced by the Michigan researchers, namely, party loyalty (or party identification) and response error (or unreliability). Once the analysis is moved to the level where it is required to explain individual party switching, any model must face the challenge these two concepts constitute.

In regard to the former, it should first be realized that the tendency of voters to repeat their vote at consecutive elections is much higher than what can be accounted for by issue position, or social class position or any other set of external factors. For example, we may have succeeded by means of a model of the type described in Chapter 2 to isolate two groups of voters, one in which 80 percent voted for the party and another in which only 10 percent did so. Applying this model to the next election we should expect, even if nobody changed their issue position or class position, that 64 percent repeated their vote for the party in the first group, and 1 percent in the last group. However, in practice we should not be surprised to find that 90 percent have repeated their vote in the first group and a considerable portion, in the last. A predisposition to vote for a particular party seems to have an effect on the vote, independent of the class position or issue position of the voter.

Thus, a concept of party loyalty is inescapable for the study of micro-level stability and change; its theoretical basis is found in social psychology. Social psychology is to a large extent a study of attitudes, their sources and

interrelations, and their behavioural consequences. From a social-psychological point of view, issue voting is the effect of an attitude upon behaviour. Hence the problem in issue voting is to set up a model to account
for the vote of the individual by reference to a set of attitudes and to study
the net effect of issue-related attitudes in such a model. For each election
survey the task was to define the relevant attitudinal dimensions which
corresponded to the issues of the election. These issue orientations would
have a number of ordered positions that largely matched the policy options that were thought available for the government.

The vote decision was seen as the terminal point of a psychological
process, which the Michigan researchers termed the "funnel of causality".
Since issues tend to occur or at least to be debated in public in connection
with elections, issue orientations were treated by the model as located late
– that is, close to the vote decision – in the funnel of causality. At that
point most voters are assumed already to have acquired other relevant
attitudes, carried over from earlier elections.

Of direct relevance for the democratic citizen's choice of party are attitudes controlling loyalty to groups and conformity with group norms. The
concept of reference groups had been proposed by psychologists Herbert
Hyman (1942) and Theodore Newcomb (1943) for denoting groups which
individuals can identify. In American elections, of course, the most plausible reference groups would be the two main parties, the Democrats and Republicans. Thus Campbell and his associates in the Michigan team suggested that party identification was a stable attitude for most American
voters, and this concept was incorporated as a cornerstone in the model of
voting behavior.

The concept of party identification should clarify what we mean by speak-
ing about continuity in voting, or the tendency of voters to repeat their vote.
According to psychological theory, orientations cause terminal behavior,
not the reverse. Therefore it is not precise to say, as we said above, that the party choice influences the issue position. Rather, what we should say is that
some partisan orientation has influenced both the party choice and the issue
orientation. The problem of reverse causality, vote influencing issue position, should be reformulated as a problem of the impact of party orientation
on both the vote and the issue position. In addition there is a possible but
weaker reverse impact of issue orientations on party identification. This is
illustrated by the following scheme.

According to this model it is important to carry out party identification
controls in assessing the extent of issue voting, because party identifiers

Figure 3.1. Impact of party identification and issue orientation on the vote

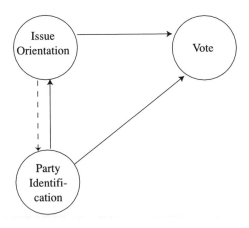

tend to take over the issue stands of their party. The impact of party identification on issue orientations is normally much stronger than the corresponding impact of social class, discussed in relation to Figure 2.1, because
parties are important actors in the policy-making process. If the impact of
party identification on issue positions is disregarded in the model, this will
show up as a spurious effect of issue positions on the vote. Hence, issue
effects will be exaggerated all the more, the greater the issue positions have
depended on party identification.

The Normal Vote Model

According to the Michigan model, issue voting was conceptualized as the
effect of issue orientations under party identification controls. The main
analytical problem was to isolate various types of effect operating on the
voter in a particular election. However, to the extent that party identification could be assumed to remain a stable individual characteristic, one may
utilize a simple method of standard calculation to estimate the effects of
any other factor on the vote.

Such a model was launched by Philip Converse in an article on "The
Concept of a Normal Vote" (1966). By a method of interpolation from a
series of American elections, Converse estimated the probability of
Democratic or Republican voting for a voter who was not influenced in
a partisan direction by short-term forces of a particular election such as
the attitude to a given issue. For each group of voters the expected vote
was computed as a long-range function of the level of party identifica-

tion, the so-called "normal vote" equation. If the vote is coded 1=Democratic and 0=Republican, while party identification is graded into five categories from 2 to -2 (2=strong Democrats, 1=weak Democrats, 0=independents, -1=weak Republicans, and -2=strong Republicans), the normal vote equation is:

Normal vote = 0.483 + 0.268 Party identification

Here, "Normal vote" represents the normal Democratic vote in a group where we have computed the average level of Democratic party identification.

The normal vote equation suffers from the same logical problem as we have encountered before, namely that it predicts a vote under 0 or over 100 percent when the variable "Party identification" takes the pure values of plus or minus two. However, this is a minor mole in the model, for these pure groups do not exist in practice when the model is applied to issue groups or social groups. The function is nearly linear for an interval of Party identification running from –1.20 to +1.20. The normal vote procedure involves three steps:

1.   Compute the mean party identification for voters at each issue position or social group for which the issue effect is to be estimated
2.   Insert these means in the normal vote equation
3.   Subtract the resulting normal vote from the actual vote.

Subtracting the normal vote from the actual vote in different issue groups or social groups, one can estimate the residual effect of an issue or social factor. And of course, applying the model to the aggregate outcome of an election we may assess how much it differs from our baseline of expectations.

It should be observed that the normal vote does not depend on assumptions of linear issue effects or on any other parameters attached to issue effects. In subtracting the normal from the actual vote in different groups, we perform a simple standard calculation. Thereby we are able to isolate effects of the issues that are non-parametric and therefore sometimes are overlooked in, paradoxically, more sophisticated models of analysis.

An example of normal vote analysis is Richard Boyd's study of the effect of the Vietnam issue on the US election in 1968. The data are presented in Table 3.1.

With regard to the "military victory" position of the Vietnam issue, the normal vote computation yields a negative issue effect. At the two right-

Table 3.1. Attitude to Vietnam policy and presidential vote in the 1968 election in the United States. Percent

Vote	Withdraw Completely						Military Victory
	1	2	3	4	5	6	7
Democratic	53%	47%	49%	45%	39%	28%	32%
Republican	38	49	51	48	56	50	46
Wallace	8	4	0	8	5	22	22
Total	99%	100%	100%	101%	100%	100%	100%
No. of Rs	169	103	100	370	133	114	241
Expected Dem.	62%	53%	53%	58%	55%	52%	59%
Issue Effect	-9%	-6%	-2%	-13%	-16%	-24%	-27%

Source: R.W.Boyd, "Popular Control of Public Policy: A Normal Vote Analysis of the 1968 Election", *American Political Science Review*, vol. 66 no. 2, 1972, p.433.

most positions the Democratic vote falls 24 and 27 percentage points short of the normal vote. According to the second and third rows, the greater share of the Democratic deficit at these positions goes to George Wallace, who receives 22 percent of the vote here.

Actually, in this case the expected Democratic vote varies little, only between 52 and 62 percent, over the seven positions on the issue. This shows that the Vietnam position of the respondents was almost uncorrelated with party identification. In that case, of course, we might as well have left out the normal vote computation and computed the vote as a function of the issue position directly. If we code the issue positions from 0=withdrawal to 1=military victory (with one step corresponding to 1/6), the regression lines are as follows:

Democratic vote = 0.54 – 0.23 Vietnam position

Republican vote = 0.44 + 0.06 Vietnam position

Wallace vote = 0.01 + 0.17 Vietnam position

The dependent variables on the left side of the equations denote the estimated frequencies of voting Democratic, Republican, or for George Wallace, among respondents with a given position on the Vietnam issue. The coefficients of the *Vietnam position* express the issue effect rather concisely: from the dovish to the hawkish position the Democratic support declines by 23 percent of the vote, 6 percent going to the Republicans but 17 percent to Wallace.

The normal vote model introduced some principles for the analysis of issue voting that are basically sound, and it meant a great leap forward despite its simplicity. But it is a question whether the rigid assumptions set up by the model are valid in practice. As noted in a fine comment by Brody and Page (1972), there are several conditions to be fulfilled.

In the first case, the model relies on the individual stability of party identification. Unlike for example generation or gender groups, and to a large extent social class membership, party identification may change in response to issue orientation. If that is the case, part of the issue effect on the vote is channeled through party identification, and this part should be added to the direct issue effect.

Second, the issue effects one observes are controlled for party identification but not for each other, thus various issue effects may to some extent duplicate one another. Thus it is still necessary to control one issue effect for all other issue effects.

Third, issues are assumed to be limited to one election; but actually they may be part of an ideological cluster of attitudes that prevail through several elections. As suggested by the examples from British voting behavior in the foregoing chapter, ideological positions strongly tend to be reference groups of voters. These groups may be just as resistant to change as party identification.

Fourth, the model is fairly easy to apply in the US electorate because its party identification is one-dimensional, running from strong Democrats via weak Democrats, independents, and weak Republicans to strong Republicans. In a multiparty system such as most European party systems, computing a normal vote soon becomes complicated and offers several options. Actually, even in the 1968 election mentioned above, the presence of the Wallace candidacy gave rise to two different versions of the normal vote analysis (Kessel 1972). According to one, Democratic identifiers voting for George Wallace were treated as short-term defectors from the democratic camp. According to the other, they should be regarded as loyal Democratic identifiers although not voting for the candidate of the majority.

The European Context

If a normal vote analysis is to be conducted for a different electorate than the American, one must start by computing the normal vote equation for the specific country. This would involve investigating a series of elections in order to eliminate those transient forces that combine with party identification to produce the election result. Furthermore, of course, survey questions measuring party identification must be available for this series of elections. These are ordinarily questions asking whether the respondent feels attached to a particular party, labels himself or herself an adherent of that party, or the like.

There have been interesting attempts to apply the normal vote model to European systems. Falter and Rattinger (1982) estimated that the normal vote would give the CDU/CSU 44 percent, the SPD 38 percent, and the FDP 8 percent of the vote in West Germany of the early 1980s. However, events of the 1980s and 1990s have changed the German party systems so as to make these estimates obsolete.

Already the 1976 anthology *Party Identification and Beyond* (Budge, Crewe and Farlie 1976) brought to light a variety of viewpoints from European researchers. There is a risk that controlling for party identification reduces the issue effect too much because in some political cultures, party identification tends to change along with the vote. In the extreme case that all party changers also change their party identification accordingly, the variance in party identification will explain the whole variance in the vote, and there will be no space left for issue effects. What, then, causes the party change? We seem to be thrown back to a position in which issues or ideologies influence both the vote and party identification. Even for the United States, it has been pointed out that there is a bias stemming from the reverse impact of issue positions on party identification (Achen 1975). In the European context, where parties tend to form "families" of the left, right, and center, these families may be the primary objects of lasting attitudes. A number of voters may then fail to identify with any party in particular, yet their voting behavior shows that they remain loyal to one particular family of parties.

The tendency of identification with left-right party families to replace simple party identification in Europe has led some researchers (such as Lewis-Beck in his comparative study, *Economics and Elections*) to apply control for left-right self-placement as a substitute for control for party identification. This solves one of the problems, but not the problem of reverse causation from issue to left-right identification. Just as there may exist a hierarchy of parties organized in blocs or families, there may be a hierarchy of issues organized in ideologies; part of the effects that we assign to one issue may therefore be the shared effects of a cluster of issues. For example, the attitude to state regulation of business almost certainly will turn out to be related to the attitudes to social equality and welfare services. By leaving out the latter from the equation, the former will take over the shared variance and become overrated. Consequently the risk of over-controlling and thereby reducing the effect one seeks to estimate will remain.

A Test on British Data

In practice, controlling for party identification certainly tends to reduce the issue effects in Britain, consistent with the Butler and Stokes study (1969, 1974). That study certainly promoted the belief that simple party identification prevailed over ideology. This view was later quantified by Franklin (1985b): across six elections, 1964-1979, he concluded that the impact of party identification on issue positions was about twice the reverse impact.

The example below (Table 3.2) shows the British Conservative vote broken down by party identification and position on the nationalization versus privatization issue. Since we saw in the foregoing chapter that the issue effects did not differ greatly from one election to the next, surveys from six elections have been combined in the analysis.

As we see, the impact of party identification, as an average for six elections, is very strong and explains a major part of the variance in the actual vote for the party. The linear regression line is

Conservative vote = .82 Party identification + .12 Privatization + .02,

Table 3.2. Conservative vote, by party identification and position on nationalization vs privatization. British elections 1964-1992.

	More nation-alization	Stay the same	More privat-ization
Conservative identification	88% (238)	93% (1878)	95% (2064)
No party identification	28% (96)	39% (310)	63% (206)
Other identification	2% (2165)	7% (2488)	17% (862)

Source: Variable PARTYID in the British election file 1964-92.

where Party identification is coded 1=Conservative, 0.5=none, and 0=other party, while Privatization is coded 1=more privatization, 0.5=stay the same, and 0=more nationalization. The correlation in the table is as high as 0.85, and the correlation with party identification alone are 0.84. Therefore, issue position makes very little difference once party identification has been verified. Still, the correlation of the vote with the issue position alone is 0.44, similar to what we saw in Chapter 2.

Thus in the linear model the effect of party identification is almost seven times as large as the effect of the issue orientation. It is seen in the table that among party identifiers the issue effect is only 7 or 15 percent, depending on whether we look at the upper or lower row. However, if a logistic regression model is applied instead of a linear model, the case for issue voting - appears somewhat stronger. The logistic model has the equation

Log odds of Conservative vote = 5.04 Party identification + 1.68 Privatization – 3.49.

The estimated issue effect according to this reckoning is about one-third of the effect of party identification. This upgrading occurs because the small percentage differences in the upper and the lower row take on a higher significance when they are converted to odds ratios.

According to the "dealignment" thesis (Dalton, Flanagan, and Beck 1984), party identification tends to decline in advanced Western democracies, opening a potential for, among other factors, increased issue voting. This conjecture is consistent with the data in Table 3.2, as party identifiers indeed seem to generate smaller issue effects than do the non-identifiers.

The influence on issue positions of party identification, perceived left-right position, opinions on issues other than the one studied, and possibly other orientations, has presented research with an ambiguity in defining the level or amount of issue voting. Some researchers cite as evidence of a rise in issue voting the fact that issue positions have become stronger correlated with party identifications. In doing so they of course show that the voters are informed about the positions of the parties on a number of - issues, and have positions themselves. But this does not address the problem of the independent impact of issues on the election outcome. Indeed, it means that such an impact must come from issues that are *unrelated* to party identification. This would be the consequence of the model presented in Figure 3.

Apparently, when we are talking about ideological issues, as in the example of Table 3.2, we should suspect issue orientations to have little direct impact on the vote. By far the greatest amount of issue/vote correlation can be ascribed to party identification, people differing in issue orientation because they differ in party identification. Translated into electoral change it means that we should expect voters to change their opinions on issues as they change partisanship, rather than the reverse. The problem is that unless we have access to panel data, we do not know to what extent voters change their party identification. Judging from cross-section data alone, we find both in Britain and Denmark that a change in the voting strength of a party is accompanied by a change in the same direction in the party's share of party identifiers. Thus the increasing Conservative vote share in 1970, from 42 to 46 percent, was accompanied by an increase in the Conservative share of identifiers from 36 to 40 percent. In 1979, the increasing Conservative vote share from 36 to 44 percent was accompanied by an increase in the share of identifiers from 35 to 39 percent. And the decline of the Labour vote from 37 percent in 1979 to under 28 in 1983 was accompanied by a decline in identifiers from 38 to 32 percent. In Denmark, the decline in the vote for the Conservative Party from 16 percent in the 1994 election to 9 percent in the 1998 election was accompanied by a decline in the Conservative share of identifiers from 16 to 12.5 percent.

To the extent that voters change their party identification in accordance with their issue positions, the issue effects in tables like Table 3.2 will be underrated. Still, the effects of party loyalty on issue positions must be judged to be at least as large as the reverse effect. The effects of party loyalty on voter opinions was anticipated in our consistency model in Chapter 1, and should not be condemned as irrational, insofar as the opinion change occurs in the direction of greater consistency with the party. It is a different matter with those voters who misrepresent the parties' positions so as to convince themselves that they are nearer to the party with which they identify than to competing parties. These may be justly termed irrational. Granberg and Holmberg (1988, 10-12) speak of three processes leading to consistency: change of party, change of opinion, or distortion of the party's position. They claim that only the third is irrational, and we agree with this view.

Response Error

The problem of opinion change at the level of the individual voter is compounded by response error. It has been demonstrated by means of panel analysis that on most issues the majority of voters are quite unstable, wavering unsystematically between positions (Converse 1964). What appears as opinion change at the individual level is better suspected to be randomness in responding to survey items about issue orientations. This is seen from the fact that these responses are unrelated to other variables in the survey, including previous responses to the same item in panel studies. As they tend to cancel one another, they do not cause change in the aggregated distributions of opinions either.

Actually, response error or low reliability in measuring issue positions seems to be the main explanation for the problem we mentioned at the beginning of the chapter, namely that opinion change was generally being more frequently observed than party switching. If the voter's opinion is stable but, unfortunately, is measured with low reliability compared with the vote, there will be a large number of *apparent* opinion changes that are not reflected in vote changes. Only a remaining few opinion changes would effectively change the vote. If we had ways of subtracting the error responses, we might still find that issue positions influenced the vote. Unfortunately this is not possible when we are dealing with single items in a survey. As we shall see in a moment, however, there are ways of pinpointing real opinion change.

How does response error affect the issue voting model? Referring to Table 2.1, one may imagine what happens if some of the respondents, unwilling to admit that they have no opinion on nationalization, shift unsystematically between the five rows in the table but all of them taking their partisanship with them. Obviously those in the upper row, where only 13 percent voted Conservative, would mix with those in the lower row, where 84 percent did so. The result would be to drive the Conservative vote in the five rows toward a common mean value; or, to be more precise, the percentage differences observed between the rows would already include this element of "noise". If these respondents could be singled out and eliminated, which unfortunately is not possible, the difference between the cells would be larger than the table indicates. But this is the same as saying that the issue effects estimated by the model are lowered by the presence of response error. Thus, the issue effect that we measure underrates the real issue effect by a factor that is proportional to the unreliability, or response error.

To Granberg and Holmberg's above-mentioned three categories of voters we might therefore add a category of irrational voters who obtained consistency between their issue position and party choice by sheer luck. On the other hand there would be consistent voters who appeared inconsistent because we were not able to measure their opinions with sufficient reliability.

It is very annoying to do research with an independent variable that is measured with a high amount of unreliability. The consequence is that one is unable to predict when the effect of that variable should occur and when it should not occur. Therefore it is plausible to attempt to improve the reliability in various ways. One way of doing this is to improve the wording of the items used in the questionnaires. Another method is to use several items, rather than a single item, to indicate the respondent's issue position. If the item is repeated in a slightly disguised way in the questionnaire, inconsistent respondents may be filtered out, or the response to several items may be combined into an index of the respondent's issue position, which will then be a more reliable estimate than any single item. A third method of taking account of response error is to build into the regression model some assumptions about measurement error. By a two-stage procedure one then estimates the "latent" or "true" issue orientations lying behind the "manifest" pattern of responses. Uncontaminated by response error, the "true" issue effects will generally be stronger than the manifest effects estimated in our example above.

Finally, a fourth way, which is the simplest and the one we used in Chapter 2, is to apply the model only to respondent groups of a certain size rather than on individual respondents. By aiming to predict the support (in percent) for a party within sizeable groups of voters, one minimizes the problem of unreliability.

The problem of unreliability has played a role in the debate about the rise in issue voting, which is supposed to have taken place at US elections during the 1950s and 1960s. The issue/vote correlations were observed to rise particularly in connection with the 1964 election (Pomper 1972; Nie with Andersen 1974), and to remain at the higher level. However, critics pointed out that the survey items used to measure respondents' issue positions had also changed between 1960 and 1964 (cf. the symposium in *American Journal of Politics*, May 1978 and Februar 1979). Therefore it was a moot question whether real change had taken place in the American electorate. If not, the conclusion would be that the bleak picture of low issue voting in the American public of the 1950s was a result of inferior measurement technique.

Party Switching and Controls for Past Vote

Almost all cross-section surveys ask the respondent to recall his or her vote at the previous election. From these recall data we can register who have switched parties, but in most cases the actual number who switch parties is underrated by the recall data because respondents tend to alter their recalled vote in the direction of their present party preference. However, many surveys nowadays include a panel of respondents who were interviewed at the previous election and such a panel of course gives more precise information about the number and identity of party switchers.

One might think that these data were ideal for the study of issue voting, especially if they ask the same questions about issue positions in both waves of the panel. One might attack the problem of controlling for partisan predispositions more directly by controlling a respondent's former vote. That is, the vote at one election may be estimated as a function of the vote in the previous election and the voter's position on one or more issues.

But caution is needed in interpreting such a function, as will be seen from the following example from a Danish panel study. In Table 3.3 the 1988 vote for the Danish bourgeois government is broken down by the respondent's position on an index of four ideological issues, and by respondent's vote in the previous election that occurred in 1987, only eight months earlier.

Table 3.3. Vote for the Danish government 1988, by 1987 vote and ideological position

Issue Position 1988	Percent Shifting 1987-1988		Total 1987	Total 1988
	From Gov. To Opp.	From Opp. To Gov.		
1 (Right)	9 (47)	50 (8)	85 (55)	85 (55)
2	9 (75)	19 (26)	74 (101)	73 (101)
3	17 (47)	7 (92)	34 (139)	2 (139)
4	18 (11)	4 (95)	10 (106)	12 (106)
5 (Left)	(0)	0 (60)	0 (60)	0 (60)

Note. N's in parentheses. To measure the ideological position, an additive index of four items was used: (1) Social reforms have gone too far in this country vs social reforms should be upheld; (2) The state should take over the banks and big industry vs banks and big industry should continue to be in private hands; (3) Differences in the standard of living are still too large in this country vs income levelling have gone far enough; and (4) Business people should be entitled to determine their own affairs to a higher degree vs The state should control and coordinate business life.

The first column indicates the percent of 1987 government voters who switched to the opposition in 1988. The figures here suggest that the government lost more voters on the left wing than on the right wing. The next column indicates the percent of 1987 opposition voters who shift to the government in 1988. These figures suggest that the government gained more voters on the right wing than on the left wing. Does this mean that the government gained voters on the right wing and lost voters on the left wing?

No! If we look at the two last columns of Table 3.3, we notice that the government vote did not change significantly from 1987 to 1988 in any of the five issue positions. Gains and losses matched each other exactly – or at least as exactly as can be expected in a sample. There was no issue effect in 1988 that was not already present in 1987.

How, then, is the illusion created that the bourgeois government lost votes on the left wing and gained votes on the right wing? Obviously by dividing the loss on the left wing by a smaller number than the loss on the right wing and reversing this procedure when it comes to the gains. A loss seems larger when taken from a small group than when taken from a large group. But actually, if the bourgeois parties should continue to be strong on the right wing and weak on the left wing, they must balance gains and losses on both wings, no matter what size these wings have. The same is true with the exchange of voters between small and large parties. In the equilibrium situation the traffic must be of the same size in both directions, which means that it must constitute a larger share of the small party's voters than of the large party's voters.

By controlling for former vote, one turns a simple process of electoral change into a difficult problem. The simple view of partisan change is illustrated by Figure 3.2.

Figure 3.2. Schematic illustration of party switching

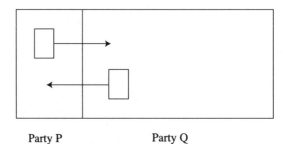

Party P   Party Q

The figure shows two parties P and Q, which are of unequal size – at least unequal within a given group of voters such as those in a particular constituency, in a particular social class, or with a particular issue position. In the absence of issues or other short-term forces, party switching will be approximately the same in both directions, as indicated by the small rectangles switching in either direction. Now, it is obvious that these rectangles, though of the same size, correspond to a much higher probability of switching away from the party which has a weak standing (P) than from a party which has a strong standing (Q). If indeed the size of the two rectangles were changed so as to be proportional to the group from which they came, we would quickly end up with two equally large parties in every voter group. Since the structure of party strength tends to continue over many elections, giving rise to approximately equal swings in the vote, there is inferential support for the theory of party identification in the aggregated data as well as in the micro-level data.

Quite apart from this basic problem of specifying the model correctly, there are other objections against using the former vote as a control variable. One objection is that such a model postulates that the vote in the previous election is a sort of baseline for the next election. However, the previous election may itself have been highly unusual, dominated by specific issues. If that were the case, the issue effects that are calculated for the new election will be a mixture of half-forgotten influences on the previous vote and the influence of new factors on the present vote.

These objections pertain to panel data as well as to vote recalls. In addition there are special objections against relying on vote recalls to reveal the respondent's former vote. Vote recalls are of course not useless, but they should be viewed with suspicion as they suffer from a systematic inclination of respondents to err in the direction of respondent's present party sympathies. Some respondents who voted Labour in 1979 but Conservative in 1983 will sometimes forget that they voted Labour four years ago. Actually, panel analysis shows that only about three-quarters of the British respondents remember their former vote correctly (Himmelweit et al. 1981, 231). Similarly, in the Netherlands, van der Eick and Niemöller found (1983, 114) for six elections that only between 82 and 69 percent remembered their former vote correctly. These figures of course include voters who do remember but do not like to reveal it to the interviewer because they are afraid it would suggest some type of personality disorder. The result will be an under-reporting of party switching that is sometimes quite damaging to our attempts to account for the real change taking place between elections.

An even more important objection against using recall data for the study of issue voting is that, even where the former vote is reported accurately, it is not possible to reconstruct the former issue position of the respondent. Thus, respondents who have gained or lost in consistency because they have changed opinion without changing their party are lost in the analysis.

The conclusion from this discussion is that if we want to study issue effects at the level of the individual voter, there is no escape from the concepts of party loyalty and response error. However, once we abandon such an ambitious project and settle for a model that works at the group level or the aggregate level, simpler solutions are available. The normal vote model offers such a simple solution. It does not attempt to put a tag on the individual voter; instead, it counts the actual number of voters at critical issue positions and compares it with the expected number.

Types of Elections

The stability of party identification and its dominant influence on the vote explains why the partisan division of the vote tends to fluctuate around a long-run equilibrium. Still, the Michigan approach recognizes the potential role of issues in affecting the outcome of presidential elections (Campbell 1966). Normal, or *maintaining*, elections are those in which short-term forces are absent or at least not sufficiently strong to sway the election outcome, so that this outcome is determined by the distribution of party identifications. Abnormal, or *deviating*, elections are those in which the distribution of party identifications yields to short-term forces running counter to party identifications. Critical, or *realigning*, elections shift the distribution of party identification so as to provide a new baseline for future elections.

This typology highlights the division into long-term and short-term attitudinal forces. Party identification is assumed to be a long-term force, durable for the lifetime in the case of most voters. Changes in party identification therefore cannot explain the different outcomes of a series of elections. These different outcomes are explained by the different balance of short-term forces. Whether an election becomes maintaining or deviating depends on this balance. Deviating elections will often feature the impact of transient issues that are cut loose from party identifications; and realigning elections may well feature a new set of issues or issue positions that come to exert a dominant and permanent effect on the vote in new generation of voters. In this interpretation, Campbell's typology applies also to parliamentary elections and to party systems in which it is more difficult to separate party identification and vote. The main problem with the notion of a realigning election is to identify, for a given election, those issues and issue positions which will dominate the next period – in retrospect, the 1945 and 1979 elections in Britain should qualify, while the prospects may differ regarding the 1997 election.

Conclusion

It seems very difficult to apply the simple regression model of issue voting, which we presented in Chapter 2, to study the electoral dynamics going on at the individual level. It is not suited to investigate in depth the question of exactly who changed their vote and for what reason. Even panel analysis gives no assurance that the model is correctly specified. Intensive controls for party identification or putatively ingrained ideologies will remove most of the direct effects of issue voting, but leaves the impression that some of the real effects are controlled out. Once we settle for the objective of measuring electoral change at the group level, however, there are much brighter prospects. The strength of a party can be seen to increase or decrease from one group of voters to the next, as can the size of these groups. On the basis of such data we may single out elections in which certain issues have affected the aggregated vote for the parties. Although this is less ambitious, it still implies that even the simple issue voting model permits a rather stringent test of various hypotheses about the causes of electoral change.

Chapter 4

Party Position and Utility

The Spatial Approach

The spatial approach has its name because of an obvious geographical analogy that visualizes the positions on an issue as ordered along a continuous dimension. Voters are distributed over that dimension with varying density, often with the highest density around the middle portion, like inhabitants living along a road that leads into a village, passes its center, and leaves it again on the other side. This gives rise to a "consumer theory" of party choice. The voters may be seen as the customers of parties or presidential candidates that are located as shops along the same road. These customers minimize their transport distances by buying in the nearest shop. In the language of Downs (1957), voters maximize their *utility* by choosing the nearest party or candidate. In their turn, parties and candidates maximize their utility by selecting their locations at places where the density of voters is high.

Such a theory requires that issue positions and utilities be measured. In respect to issue positions, the intended rationality of the model seems to imply that the issue positions of the parties be objectively measured, in the sense that there is general agreement on each party's position. If some voters place the party differently from other voters, they can claim that to them the party is very close, while others would say that another party might be closer. This introduces a complexity in the model that we shall deal with at the end of the chapter.

Furthermore, it is required that the issue positions be measured on equal interval scales. If positions 1 and 2 on an issue are much closer to each other than positions 2 and 3, a voter at position 2 would always prefer a party that is situated at position 1 to a party that is situated at position 3. If the two distances were equal, that voter would prefer the two parties equally. Therefore, at least the positions must be translated into metric positions if the model is to work correctly.

The "Nearest Party" Hypothesis

For a crude test of the "nearest party" hypothesis we may, for a moment, bypass the concept of utility. If we have a valid measure of the distance between the voters' issue positions and those of the parties, we may group the voters according to which party is the nearest. That party is simply assumed to have the highest utility. The hypothesis then predicts which voters will vote for which party. And of course, the aggregated outcome of the election is predicted in the same process.

In order to test the hypothesis we need to place the voters and the parties on the same issue scale. The foregoing chapters have suggested how voter positions are measured, but not how to measure party positions. One research-stimulating impact of the spatial model has been the efforts to *measure* the parties' positions on different issues and on the left-right scale. These positions can be established by means of sources outside the electoral surveys: roll calls in the legislature when issues are debated; mentions of the issue in party programs or election platforms; or assessment by experts or journalists. In such cases the spatial model links electoral research to the study of political elite behavior.

But information on the parties' positions may also come from the survey respondents acting as judges. In most modern election surveys, the respondents are asked to indicate the parties' positions on a number of issues, as well the respondents' own positions. From the former data one can compute a mean position of each party across all these issues. From the latter, one can then compute the distance between the respondent and each party.

A test along these lines spells out the failure of the "nearest party" hypothesis, at least in Britain. Heath, Jowell, and Curtice (1985, 97) sum up "what the results might have been" in the 1983 election if the outcome had conformed to the consumer theory. Looking at which party was the closest for the individual respondent on an index of five issues that were prominent in the campaign, they conclude that the Conservatives should get 35 percent, the Alliance 31, and Labour 35 percent of the vote in their sample. Actually the election ended on 42, 25, and 28 percent, respectively, for the three major parties. Thus the nearest-party calculation would predict a tie between Conservative and Labour, whereas in fact the Conservatives won by a comfortable margin of 14 percent of the vote.

Fourteen years later the vote swung dramatically toward Labour. Was the 1997 election closer than the 1983 election to the nearest party hypothesis? In terms of the voters' self-placement and their placement of the parties on a left-right scale, the situation in the English sample (that is, excluding the Scottish) is illustrated in Figure 4.1. Those at positions 0-4 are closest to the Labour position at 3.82; those at positions 5-6 are closest to the Liberal position at 4.71; and those at position 7-10 are closest to the Conservative position at 7.37. These three groups contained 33, 41, and 26 percent of the sample, respectively.

However, in practice Labour took 40 percent of the votes as against the Liberal Democrats' 18 percent and the Conservatives' 30 percent (the remaining 4 percent going to various small parties). This outcome was a result of a sizeable fraction of the centrist vote choosing Labour even though they were nearer to the Liberal Democratic position. Actually, a breakdown of the three voter groups in Figure 4.1 shows that only 53 percent of the sampled respondents choose the nearest party according to this model.

In Denmark the nearest party hypothesis underestimates the vote for the two largest parties, the Social Democratic with 36 percent and the Liberal with 24 percent of the vote in the 1998 election. Both of these parties are flanked by smaller parties that, according to the hypothesis, should cut off support for the large parties from major segments of the left-right axis. This does not occur to a significant extent, however. Thus the nearest-

Figure 4.1. 1997 Vote in England predicted from nearest party hypothesis

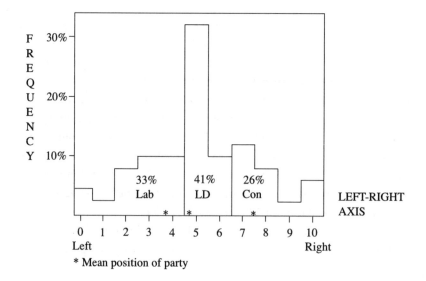

party hypothesis is easily refuted in the Danish party system, as it is the British.

Hence the objection against the Downsian perspective: many voters are not "issue distance" voters. One reason for this was indicated in the foregoing chapter. Many party identifiers place themselves nearer to another party, yet vote for the party they feel attached to. Another reason is suggested later in the present chapter: centrist parties like the British Liberal Democrats or the Danish Radical Liberals attract fewer voters than expected by the Downs model because neutral center positions have little utility for a voter, no matter what the voter's own position is. A third reason, which will be discussed in Chapters 6 and 7, is that factors like the competence and performance of a party in government may override the voter's issue position.

Right from the inception of the spatial model, critics have raised doubts about the empirical validity of the model, its verisimilitude. A central member of the Michigan team, Donald Stokes, in reviewing (1963) the potentialities of the spatial model, found some basic points to criticize. One problem is that the model presupposes that all voters share the same issue dimension – or, when the model is generalized to more than one dimension, the same issue space. *Political Change in Britain* (Butler and Stokes 1969, 200-5) points out that the preference order of many British respondents was inconsistent with the conventional order of the three main parties from left to right. But above all, the whole concept of policy position, Stokes claimed, was of limited value since many issues were not position issues but *valence* issues. Everybody is against unemployment, against inflation, in favor of economic growth, et cetera; the campaign is about how important the problem is and who can tackle it more competently.

This is an important objection against the spatial model, and will be taken up in Chapters 6 and 7. But to abandon the spatial model on these grounds is like throwing out the baby with the bath water. From the beginning of Chapter 2 we have seen that it makes sense to study the party choice as a function of issue proximity or distance. For example, in the case of Britain, 1992, we saw in Table 2.1 that at each distance from the positions of the parties, the Conservative Party was superior to the other two in conquering votes. Yet, for both the Conservatives and Labour, the proximity theory was useful in predicting variations in the vote division associated with voter positions on an issue. The reason why the "nearest party" hypothesis failed was not that voters are not distance voters, but that they also take into account other factors such as competence in government.

Mediated Issue Positions

One variant of the nearest party model requires only that the voters make judgment about which party is closest to them on different issues. Thereby the positions of the voter and of the parties on various issues need not be recorded. For example, the British 1983 survey included data on six issues: defence, unemployment, inflation, health and social services, nationalization, and law and order. For each issue the respondent was asked which party's view came closest to the respondent's own view. In his account of the election outcomes, Crewe utilizes these data as one component of issue voting. He computes the Conservative or Labour lead on each issue, showing that the Conservative position was preferred by the majority on the defence and inflation issues, while Labour was leading on the unemployment and health service issues (Crewe, 1985). Dunleavy and Husbands make use of similar data to substantiate their account of issue voting in 1983 in the case of unemployment (Dunleavy and Husbands, 1985, 158) and defence (p. 164).

Other researchers have expressed skepticism about the value of these items, suspecting them of being leading and merely restating party preferences (see for example Heath, Jowell and Curtice 1985, 90). The problem is that the wording cues many respondents, especially those who have little knowledge of the parties' positions, to contend that their own party is closest to their positions. The item *mediates* the association between the party and the issue position. However, if partisan predispositions completely determined policy evaluations, such evaluations would aggregate to the same marginals irrespective of the policy area concerned. The same number of respondents would say that the Conservative Party was the best party on different policy issues. This is usually not the case. The parties' *policy images* turn out to differ greatly, a phenomenon utilised in the salience and performance models, which we shall review in Chapters 6 and 7.

The "closest party" items may be viewed as rudimentary position variables with which to investigate an electorate that is not expected to have very autonomous views on issues. Based on the information from the above six items one might construct six primitive position, or proximity, variables, all of the dummy variable form: 1=closest to Conservative party, 0=closest to one of the other parties. These may be inserted individually in the issue distance function:

Conservative vote = $a + b_1$ Proximity on issue 1 + ... + b_6 Proximity on issue 6

This function will estimate the effect of being closest to the party on each of the six issues. Alternatively, a more general index of issue proximity may be constructed by counting the *number of issues* on which the party is seen as closest. The Conservative vote is of course then hypothesized to rise in rough proportion to the value of that index from 0 to 6. The same procedure can then be repeated for the other parties.

The issue effects b_1 to b_6 are in this case constant parameters to be computed for a cross-section survey. This means that differences between voters in their support for a party will be due to differences in some of the six proximity variables. As in the position model, some voters may vote for the party because they feel close to its policy on issue 1, others because they feel close to its policy on issue 2, and so forth. If the model is aggregated over all voters, it will suggest how the outcome of the election would be affected if either (a) the policy images of the parties were different than they are at present (for example, if more voters came to see Labour as the closest in a certain issue), or (b) if a particular issue area came to be seen as more important than it is at present (for example, if the issues on which Labour was seen as the closest party became the decisive issues of the election). Thus a party gains voters by being in tune with public opinion on important issues. By this logic, British researchers can claim that the Conservative Party won in 1983 by being close to the majority of voters on most of the leading issues.

Party Strategy

An important property of the spatial model is that it treats the relationship between the voters and the parties/candidates as a game in which all of them are actors who can move from one position to another, or in the language of game theory, change their strategies. Issue proximity implies that the issue effect is predicted to depend on changes in the parties' positions in addition to that of the voters. A change in a party's position toward the left on an issue, other things being equal, will increase its attractiveness among respondents to the left of the party, because they are now closer to the party. It will decrease its attractiveness among voters on the right, as their distance to the party has increased. These votes will of course be offset by gains for the other parties or losses to other parties. Therefore a change in any party's position will affect the vote of all parties.

In regard to party strategy, Downs suggested that in a two-party system the parties, though they may have originated on each pole of the main left-

right axis, would be forced by the competition for voters to gravitate toward the position of the median (middle) voter on the issue dimension. By
moving toward the median voter a party will gain the voters that are located between the parties. Eventually the two parties would end up side by
side in the center, their policies indistinguishable from one another. The
position of the median voter would become the policy of the government.
In theory, if one party copied all except one policy position from the other
party, and if it were nearer to the median voter on the one remaining issue,
it would win the election!

For a two-party system or a system with two dominant government alternatives, the model contains the message that it is dangerous to leave the
political center in an attempt toward ideological clarity or "purity". Consequently it also provides a simple explanation of why the Democratic and
the Republican Party tend to mirror each other's policy stands. It is consistent with the theory that bourgeois parties declared a consensus on welfare politics during the 1960s. It also explains why social democratic parties during the 1990s have integrated free-market stances and tougher stances on crime into their programs. Ironically, the model starts out by relying
on issue effects to explain the vote, but ends up by postulating the disap-
pearance of issue effects.

However, the succession of electoral swings suggest that for various reasons, the two leading parties or partisan blocs do not always gravitate toward the median voter opinion. One reason might be that the party leaders
are committed to a particular ideology that prevents them from vote max-
imizing. Another reason is that the reward and punishment mechanism
that is built into the model only works with a certain lag. As aggregated
public opinion changes toward the left or right, the median voter's position changes too, causing a swing in favor of one or the other party, and it
may take some elections before the losing party has identified the cause of
its loss. We may find such a lag in Labour's reaction to the rightward shift
in British opinion in the late 1970s on the issue of nationalization and
other ideological issues. This shift led to defeats for the Labour party both
in 1979 and 1983, because the party was unable to adapt to it. On the other
hand, the Conservative party may well have over-reacted to the new ideological winds in 1983, thereby giving the Liberal Democratic party a
chance to dominate the political center.

The center-seeking strategy is only one among several strategies the parties may employ. More common is the tendency of parties to stay at their
issue positions. The ideological differences between the Conservative Party

and the Labour Party have been relatively constant over the years, as we saw in Chapter 2. This fact suggests that issue distances are not only perceived by the voters as real; they are also deeply ingrained features of party systems.

Proximity and Utility

The measurement of party positions is one novel idea characterizing the spatial model relative to the Michigan model. Another new idea was that about the parties having different *utility* for the voter. Thus a voter's relationship to a party is not simply a choice between voting or not voting for it; it may be thought of as a continuous variable ranging from the highest to lowest possible utility. We may hypothesize utility in the proximity theory to be a negative function of the voter's distance from the party:

$$\text{Utility} = a - b^* \, |\text{Voter position} - \text{Party position}|.$$

Here, *Utility* stands for the utility, for voters located at *Voter position* on an issue, of a party that is located at *Party position*. The difference *Voter position – Party position* is taken in the absolute sense, without sign.

Compared with the simple model in Chapter 2, the utility model differs on several points. First, utilities are not the same as the vote probabilities. The translation of utilities into votes is not straightforward, since the utility of one party for a voter is independent of the utilities of other parties for the same voter: the positions of these other parties do not enter the model. For example, it is possible for a respondent to rate two parties or candidates highly, but not to vote for both of them (except in rare election systems). Therefore, in theory the utility model can be applied to one party at a time without bothering about the disturbance caused by the positions of other parties.

How can utilities be measured? This can be done in many different and imaginative ways. In the case of Britain, Himmelweit et al. (1981, 118), computing Downs' "consumer model" for several British elections, counted the number of issues (out of 21) for which a given party had more utility than other parties to the voter. The respondent had to say that the issue was *desirable* and *more* likely to be implemented by the given party, or *undesirable* and *less* likely to be implemented by that party. Utility scores thus ranged from –21 to +21. The researchers then went on to classify their respondents as expected Conservative, Labour, or Liberal voters according to which party had the highest utility for them. They were rather successful in predicting a Conservative or Labour vote, but less so in predicting a Liberal vote. Hence, they end up with the same problem as the one that caused Heath and his colleagues to discard the consumer model.

In the approach we shall follow, utilities of different parties are operationalised by the voter's attitudes to different parties. A minimal measure of it is obtained by letting the respondents indicate their feeling for each major party on a five-point scale from "strongly like" to "strongly dislike". This method is employed in for example the British questionnaires. A more differentiated measure is provided by sympathy ratings of parties, party leaders and presidential candidates. These items have been used by the Michigan surveys since the beginning of the 1970s and have spread from them to surveys in other countries, as they have turned out to offer a rich field for analysis. The items ask the respondents to rate the party or candidate according to how well the respondent likes that party or candidate, using a sort of thermometer that runs from +100 to -100 degrees.

Hence utility is translated into feelings, a procedure that seems to carry some problems with it because a voter may have a cool perception of a party's or candidate's use value without having a similar positive affect toward that party or candidate, or vice versa. The attitude toward a party has an affective component that the utility concept does not have. This component is brought to the fore in the concept of party identification. Therefore, when we measure utility as an attitude, the risk is that voters start out with high "utility" and afterwards try to make their issue position consistent with their party's position. In brief, the proximity formula above, though it has the appearance of a rational-choice deduction, tells us nothing about the underlying causality.

Having estimated the utility of different parties for respondents who are placed at different positions, the next step would be to demonstrate that there is a high probability that the respondents choose the party with the greatest utility. For a group of electors defined by their issue positions, one may, for example, hypothesize that the vote division between any two parties is a linear function of the difference between their utilities. However, the theory at this point is little developed. In the example below, we concentrate on the determinants of utility.

In respect to the right-hand side of the equation, which issues should be chosen, and how should we compute the overall distance between the voter and the party? Concerning the former, in theory the issues should be weighted according to some formula expressing their importance to the voter. This brings up a problem that we shall not deal with until Chapter 6.

Concerning the latter question, the overall distance may be computed as Euclidean distance according to the law of Pythagoras, or it may be computed as "city-block" distance by adding up the distances on all (important) issue dimensions. In the following we shall pursue the city-block method.

Testing the Proximity/Utility Model

British data. As an example of applying the proximity/utility model, we turn to the British 1992 survey, in which the respondents were asked to indicate their position and the positions of the parties on four issue scales, which ranged from 1 to 11 (questions 35 to 38):

1. Some people feel that getting people back to work should be the government's top priority. Other people feel that keeping prices down should be the government's top priority.

2. Some people feel that government should put up taxes a lot and spend much more on health and social services. Other people feel that government should cut taxes a lot and spend much less on health and social services.

3. Some people feel that government should nationalize many more private companies. Other people feel that government should sell off many more nationalized industries.

4. Some people feel that government should make much greater efforts to make people's income more equal. Other people feel that government should be much less concerned about how equal people's incomes are.

The mean positions assigned to the parties over these four scales were 3.12 for the Labour Party, 4.53 for the Liberal Democratic Party, and 7.45 for the Conservative Party, while the mean position of the respondents themselves was 4.44. Since the midpoint of the scale is 6, the respondents were somewhat tilted to the left.

With respect to party sympathies or "utilities", the survey asked (question 14) for the respondents' attitude to the parties on a scale from 1=strongly in favour, to 5=strongly against. In the present analysis these are recoded into "temperatures", from +100=strongly in favour, over +50=in favour, 0=neither in favour nor against, -50=against, to -100=strongly against. The average rating of the parties was +3.6 for the Conservative Party, +7.9 for the Liberal Democratic Party, and –4.9 for the Labour Party. Thus, in spite of the tilting toward the left, the Labour Party received the least sympathy. And though the Liberal Democrats got only 17 percent of the vote of the sample, as against 45 percent to the Conservative Party and 38 percent to Labour, it received the most sympathy. Hence it is seen that insofar as aggregate scores are concerned, closeness to the average voter's issue position does not guarantee sympathy, and sympathy does not guarantee votes. The party which is shown the highest sympathy usually gets the respondent's vote; but when sympathies are aggregated, a party may be well liked without being the most preferred for many of the voters. Whether in single candidate election systems or in proportional represen tation, being the second best party does not count.

The relation of sympathy to issue position is summarised in Table 4.1.

The sympathy for the Conservative Party increases in a linear way from left to right, and the sympathy for the Labour Party decreases in a linear way though at a considerably lower level. The sympathy for the Liberal Democratic Party varies less violently, and it has a maximum in the center or just left of the center. Recalling that the mean position of the Conservative party as assessed by the sample was 7.45, we at once spot a problem associated with the proximity theory: the sympathy does not culminate at the party's position but at the extreme right. The same calamity occurs for the Labour Party: the sympathy reaches maximum on the extreme left rather than at the party's position, 3.12. Only for the Liberal Democratic Party, the maximum coincides with the party's position, 4.53.

Nevertheless, distances tend to predict sympathy fairly well. Regressing the sympathy scores of the individual voters on their absolute distances (over the 11-points issue scale) from the party positions according to Equation 4.1 we find:

Table 4.1. Sympathy for British parties 1992, by respondent's average position on four issues. Sympathy scores between +100 and –100.

Respondent Position	Mean sympathy for party			
	Cons.	Labour	Lib.Dem.	N
1-2.75 (Left)	-39	33	7	(394)
3-4.75	-7	4	13	(614)
5-6.75	32	-37	11	(428)
7-8.75	59	-53	-4	(171)
9-11 (Right)	77	-82	-23	(31)

Conservative sympathy = 64 – 19 Distance from Conservative Party   (r = - .51)
Labour sympathy = 26 – 18 Distance from Labour Party   (r = - .41)
Liberal/Democratic sympathy = 18 – 6 Distance from
   Liberal/Democratic Party   (r = -.15)

for the three parties, where *Distance* stands for absolute distances. It is seen
that all three effect coefficients are negative, as they should be, but the effect and correlation coefficients are rather small in the case of the Liberal
Democratic party. These equations are graphed in Figure 4.2.

Figure 4.2. Sympathy for British parties, by respondent's absolute distance
      from the party's position on four issues (1994 election).

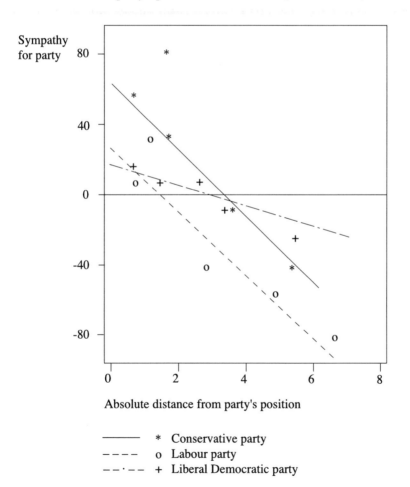

This pattern shows one important difference from the pattern we observed in Table 2.1: despite its failure to win votes, the Liberal Democratic Party receives broad sympathy. Otherwise the similarity between the two patterns is surprising as the issues are different, attitude or utility has replaced the vote, and the assumed positions of the parties have been replaced by mean positions perceived by the survey respondents. As was the case when we studied the issue/vote relation in Table 2.1, the support for the Conservative Party is larger than for the Labour Party at each distance, and the two lines are almost parallel. The line for the Liberal Democratic Party is much flatter than for the two wing parties; but overall, the Liberal Democratic Party is as popular as the two larger parties.

Proximity theory does not explain why the support for center parties is less responsive to issue distances than is the support for wing parties. Neither does it explain why the Liberal Democrats are unable to translate their high popularity or "utility" into a corresponding voting strength. For many voters, however, the Liberal Democratic Party is the second choice – and this does not count, whether in single member constituencies or under proportional representation.

Danish data. In a multiparty system such as the Danish it would be cumbersome to test the theory on all parties, even though this would provide a number of independent tests of the theory. However, since the proximity theory does not state that the issue effect should differ from one party to another, it may as well be tested in one pooled regression analysis in which all the major parties are jumbled. The result is an effect of distance on sympathy, or utility, that applies to all parties rather than one party. However, a slightly more advanced computer programme is required because in a pooled regression analysis each respondent is not treated as one case but several cases, one for each party that the respondent evaluates.

In the example below (Table 4.2) from the Danish 1994 survey the regression lines were computed from aggregated data rather than individual-voter data. The sympathy measures again run from +100 to –100 degrees.

The first column of Table 4.2 indicates the mean position of six parties on the issue of free market versus state regulation of business. The parties are ordered from left to right, and the positions range from -2 to +2. The next five columns indicate the mean sympathy shown for these parties by respondents who occupy different positions on the issue. For the three

Table 4.2. Sympathy for six parties, by respondent's position on the state re-
gulation/free market issue, in the Danish 1994 election. Sympathy scores between -100 and 100.

Respondents' Positions on the State/Market Issue

Party	Posi-tion	State Re-gulation -2	-1	0	1	Free Market 2
Soc. People's P	-1.21	9	25	-3	-31	-52
Social Dem	-.47	29	36	28	2	-16
Radical Lib	.03	-9	11	8	-12	-30
Conservative	.95	-43	-21	1	28	32
Liberal P	1.13	-50	-30	-6	37	45
Progress P	1.40	-84	-68	-46	-25	-11
No. of Rs		38	151	729	511	239

first parties, the highest sympathy is scored among respondents at position -1, the moderate leftist position. Here the Socialist People's party receives a rating of +25 "degrees", while the Social Democratic party receives
a rating of +36 degrees and the small Radical Liberal party, a rating of +11
degrees. For the last three parties, the highest rating is given by respondents who place themselves at position +2, the extreme right position.
Here the Conservative party receives +32 and the Liberal party, +45 degrees
of sympathy. It is worth noting that the proximity theory seems to work
better in the Danish case than in the British, especially in the case of the
Social Democratic Party.

In the pooled regression analysis it is of course possible to add dummy
variables for different parties. The theoretical argument for this procedure
is that some parties – for example, those having been in government – have
more credible and responsible positions than other parties. In the above example it is noteworthy that the rating of the Progress party is much lower
than ratings of the other parties and comes no higher than –11 at the right-
most position. For this reason we shall include in the regression model a
dummy variable indicating evaluation of the Progress party. The pattern of
observations is shown in Figure 4.3, and the regression line is indicated
below the diagram.

Figure 4.3. Distance from party position on state/market issue and sympathy for the Danish parties (1994 election)

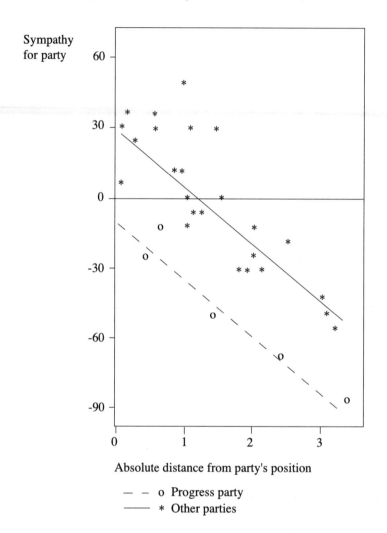

Regression line: Sympathy = 29 – 24 |Voter position – Party position| – 40 Progress party evaluation

The fit with the proximity model is rather good, with a multiple correlation coefficient of R=0.89, for these 30 observations, when the dummy variable for the Progress party is included in the model. However, the proximity theory here demonstrates another weakness: it does not account for the fact that some parties are definitely much less popular than others at a given issue distance.

We now turn to a model that employs a different perspective on the relation between issue positions and sympathy for parties.

Directional Theory

The proximity theory has a theoretical elegance that for many years made it the dominant theory in spite of its lack of fit with emperical data; but in 1989 it was challanged by the directoral theory (Rabinowith and Macdonald 1989). Directional theory takes account of the social-psykological theory that attitudes are products of subject and stimulus affects, either of which can be more or less positive, more or less negative, or nonexistent. To the extent that a party and a voter are on the same side on an issue – both positive, or both negative – the party will have positive utility for the voter, whereas it will have negative utility when the party and the voter are on different sides of the issue. When either the voter or the party are at the neutral midpoint of an issue, the party will have zero utility. Consequently, when the voter position and the party position are measured in terms of positive or negative *deviations* from the neutral midpoint, the relationship is captured in the formula *Utility = Voter deviation*Party deviation*. The term on the right-hand side is the so-called scalar product of the positions. However, the directional theory also explicitly assumes that a party that is too extreme suffers a penalty for taking an irresponsible issue position. The regression equation to be estimated therefore takes the form:

Utility = a + b Voter deviation*Party deviation – Penalty.

This expresses that the utility of the party for the voter is a positive function of the scalar product of the voter's and the party's positions on the issue.

The difference between the proximity and directional models stems from a controversy over how to interpret positions on an issue scale. The proximity model assumes that voters think in terms of distances and respond to items accordingly. The directional model assumes that voters basically think – or, perhaps, rather feel – in terms of dichotomies: if they are at all engaged in an issue, they will tend to see it as having two opposite poles, and they will tend to be positive toward one and negative toward the other. Different positions on the same side – between "partly agree" or "strongly agree", for example – indicate intensity of feeling, not positions in the geographical sense. According to the geographical interpretation, distances are always positive (and always incur negative utility). By contrast, the directional theory assumes that positions and utilities can be negative or positive, hence its name.

In comparing the two models, one notes that if the absolute distance *Voter position Party position* is squared, it will contain the scalar product *Voter deviation*Party deviation*, plus something else. So in a technical sense the difference between the two models need not be as great as it looks at first glance. Indeed, for a party taking an extreme position on the issue, the two models lead to the same prediction, namely that the closer the voter is to the party, the more the voter will like it. But for a party taking a more moderate stand, the two models differ in their predictions. The proximity model here states that the utility of the party will be highest for those voters who are at the party's position and decline in both directions. The directional model states that a moderate party will have a gently sloping linear utility curve. A party right in the political center will have no utility for the voter no matter where the voter stands on the issue.

Some attempts have been made to elaborate a model of utility that combines the proximity and directional models. "Mixed" models that were superior to either of the pure models have been proposed, the most sophisticated ones having been proposed by Merrill and Grofman (1999). It has been hypothesized, for example, that well-informed voters tend to follow the proximity model and less informed voters, the directional model, in displaying sympathy for the parties (Merrill, 1995; Maddens 1996). But at least for Norway and the United States, this peace proposal has been rejected (Macdonald, Rabinowitz and Listhaug 1995): educated voters produced higher correlations than less educated in both models, but without altering the superiority of the directional model.

Party strategy. The party strategies recommended by directional theory differ from the Downsian strategy earlier mentioned. According to directional theory, parties should move away from the center because voters on either side of the center will prefer the most extreme party on their side. It does not matter that this party will also be the most despised by voters on the other side. If we aggregate the utility for a given party over all voters, it will be a simple product of the party's position (center distance) and the mean opinion on the issue. If the mean is on the side of the party – for example, public opinion is leftist and the party is left of center – there will be a net positive utility for the party. Consequently the party should move to the extreme position (short of the penalty zone) in order to maximize its aggregated utility. If on the other hand the mean opinion is against the party, the party should move into the center so as to minimize its negative utility (we assume that it is not at liberty to completely reverse its position).

The theory does not say where the zone of responsibility ends, and penalty begins; it is left to empirical investigation to ascertain this point. A preliminary test for Norway and Sweden (Rabinowitz, Macdonald and Listhaug 1991) suggests that parties tend to locate themselves at some distance from the center or, if they remain in the center, tend to lose voters.

There may be a weakness in the "zone of responsibility" notion. But as we have just witnessed in the Danish case, the proximity model is not likely to work either if extreme parties are treated on a par with moderate ones. The initial tests of the two models usually came out on the side of the directional model. Rabinowitz and Macdonald (1989) showed that for the United States, its fit with the data on six issues was far superior to the fit of the proximity model. For a number of European elections, it has been shown that parties generally attain their maximum popularity (sympathy) near the end of the most important issue dimension, consistent with the assumptions of directional theory. However, there are exceptions, two of which happen to be the Danish Social Democratic and Radical Liberal parties (Listhaug, Rabinowitz and Macdonald 1994).

The directional model predicts that the more extreme the party, the steeper the slope of its utility function. We might call this a polarization hypothesis. The proximity model has no such prediction. On the contrary, according to the proximity logic a distance of one unit is a distance of one unit, no matter where it occurs on the scale. Herein lies an interesting possibility of confronting the models. Unfortunately this possibility is almost never harnessed as the testing normally proceeds for one party at a time, so that variations between parties are not investigated. In comparing the models one party at a time, testing the directional theory simply means checking that the sympathy is a linear function of the voter's position (provided that the slope has the right sign).

A more complete test of the directional model requires evidence that a group of voters at a given position are more positive toward an extreme (but responsible) party than toward a moderate party on their own side of the center. And similarly, the proximity model requires that a group of voters at a given position assign utility to different parties according to the distance from these parties. As observed by Westholm (1997) the test should be intrapersonal, not interpersonal. It is the voter who chooses among the parties; it is not the case that the party chooses the nearest voters, for all voters have the same utility for the party whether they come from near or far. However, interpersonal tests are simpler to execute by standard computer programs.

British data. If we execute a party-by-party regression of sympathy for the British parties on the voter's deviations from the neutral position (position 6), the following results are obtained:

Conservative sympathy = 30 + 17.0 Voter deviation   (with r = .52)
Labour sympathy = − 32 + 15.9 Voter deviation   (with r = .50)
Liberal/Democratic sympathy = 6 + 1.8 Voter deviation   (with r = .08),

First, if we compare the fit with the corresponding equations for the proximity theory, we find that the correlation is slightly higher for the Conservative Party and substantially higher for the Labour Party, whereas for the Liberal Democratic Party it is even lower than that resulting from proximity theory. The above correlations are of course exactly the same whether or not the voter position is multiplied by the party position.

Next, by comparing the three parties with each other, we note that voters at the neutral point, *Voter deviation* = 0, have a positive attitude to the Conservative Party but a negative attitude to Labour. This is not predicted by the directional theory, which predicts that all the lines go through the point (0,0).

Furthermore, the coefficient of *Voter deviation* is considerably higher for the Conservative Party and the Labour Party than for the Liberal Democratic Party, where it almost vanishes. Directional theory hypothesizes that the issue effect will be proportional to the party's deviation from the neutral mean. The placement of the three parties is, as we recall, 7.45, 3.12, and 4.53 for the Conservative, Labour, and Liberal-Democratic parties respectively. Converted to deviations from position 6, they become +1.45, −2.88 and −1.47, respectively. Consequently we would expect the slope coefficient to be almost twice as high for the Labour Party than for each of the other two parties. However, this is evidently not true.

The directional theory is not a good guide to predicting the magnitude of the issue effect in this case. The theory seems to go wrong in its conceptualization of "the neutral point" of the issue index. If we had been permitted to move the neutral point somewhat to the left, from 6 to about 4.5,

or approximately to the Liberal Democratic position, we would have succeeded better in matching the negative and positive differences with the
issue effects in the above equations.

Danish data. In the case of the Danish data, we observe from Table 4.2
that the three leftist parties in the upper half of the table do not obey
the assumption of the directional theory, namely, that the sympathy for
the party rises or falls in a linear fashion from one end of the issue to the
other. For the rightist parties in the lower half, this assumption seems
valid. To get an overall measure of the fit we may, as with the proximity
theory, test the directional theory in a pooled analysis of all parties
simultaneously. Thereby we shall test not only the linearity but also the
hypothesis that the coefficient of the scalar product *Voter deviation*Party
deviation* is the same for all parties. As in the case of the proximity test, it
will be assumed that the most extreme party, the right-wing Progress
party, is penalized for being too extreme to be considered a responsible
party. We do not, however, insert dummy variables to control for utility
differences among other parties. If a dummy variable indicating evaluations of the Progress party is added to the equation, the result of the
analysis is:

Sympathy = 3 + 19 Voter deviation*Party deviation – 53 Progress party
evaluation (with R = .89)

The degree of fit on the aggregated level, as indicated by the multiple correlation coefficient, is exactly the same as in the proximity model. However,
a satisfying property of the above equation is the fact that the intercept is
only 3 "degrees", or close to zero. A plot of the data and regression function is shown in Figure 4.4. We observe that sympathy for the Progress party (o) is now more than fifty degrees below that predicted for the other five
parties (*).

It appears that even in the Danish party system, where the sympathies
for the parties are not linear, the directional theory is superior to the proximity theory when the test is conducted on the whole party system simultaneously.

However, the directional theory seemingly has a weakness relative to the
proximity theory in accounting for in-between "third parties" such as the
British Liberal Democratic Party, or more especially, the Danish Social
Democratic party. It follows from directional theory that to voters in the

Figure 4.4. Sympathy for party, by product of party position and voter position on the state/market issue (Denmark, 1994)

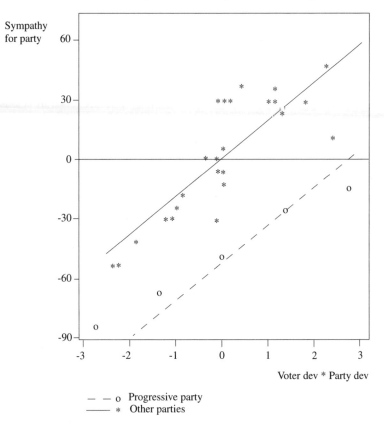

neutral center position, the utility is zero for all parties. So, if all parties are
equally good or bad, and if the voter has to choose, it becomes a random
decision which party is chosen. But if so, the center party gains an advantage at the center position compared with other positions, for in other
positions there is no similar random choice: either the left or the right
party will have a positive utility. To my knowledge nobody has ventured
into a model which may test this possibility.

Real and Perceived Party Position

In testing the proximity and directional models against one another, a
party's position is treated as a constant, common to all voters and therefore independent of the individual voter's position. If respondents' assess-

ment of the parties' positions is available in the surveys, their mean value for each party can be defined as that party's "real" or "true" position.

The sensible argument has been put forward that, since respondents do not know the mean, or "true", position of the parties, they must act on the positions which they perceive the parties to have; thus it is these individual perceptions that should be used in our models (Merrill 1995). It is obviously correct social psychology to claim that voters must act on what they perceive, rather than on what other voters perceive. Furthermore, the fact that some voters perceive the party positions differently than the rest may be valuable pieces of information for understanding why they fail to conform to the proximity or directional models in these simple versions. According to the proximity theory, if they have a preference for a particular party, simple rules of selective perception or cognitive consistency will predict that they will tend to draw that party nearer to their own position. Perhaps to a lesser extent, they will also tend to push away parties that they do not like from their own position. If they follow directional theory, they should push a party they like outward to the point where it crosses the zone of acceptability.

Hypothetically, therefore, the issue effect in both models should be larger and fit the data better when perceived party position replaces "true" position. The study of the 1983 British election (Heath, Jowell and Curtice 1985, 101) confirms this tendency in the case of the proximity model. In placing the Conservative party on an unemployment/inflation scale, respondents who preferred fighting inflation rather than unemployment tended to place the Conservative party as also fighting inflation if they had voted Conservative (53%) but not if they had voted Labour (23%). However, at the other end, respondents who would like the government to fight unemployment placed the Conservative Party as fighting inflation if they had voted Labour (58%) but not if they had voted Conservative (25%).

In theory one can combine true and perceived position postulating that some persons, who perceive the party's position to be different from its true position, must utilize the perceived position as a basis for estimating the utility of the party. This model can be written as follows:

True distance from party	$\rightarrow$	Perceived distance	$\rightarrow$	Utility of party

The true distance is here reflected in the perceived distance, but with some inaccuracy. Those who perceive their distance from the party as being greater or smaller than it actually is, adjust the utility of the party accordingly.

This model seems to have a reasonable fit with the data. In an additive index of the four issues mentioned above, we find a fairly high correlation between the true distance from the Conservative Party and the perceived distance from that party ($r=0.56$ in 1998). The correlation between the perceived distance and the utility of, or attitude to, the Conservative Party, is also rather high ($r=0.53$). Multiplying these coefficients yields 0.30. This takes care of the major part of the total correlation between the true distance and the utility, which is $r=0.40$.

If the same model is applied to the Labour Party, this is even more true. The first link has an $r=0.52$ and the second link, an $r=0.39$. The product of these correlations is 0.20, not much lower than the coefficient of 0.24 for the correlation between true distance and utility.

But the suspicion remains that sympathy toward the party may independently reinforce these causal paths. From the party identification model in Chapter 3 we may expect the attitude toward the party to affect both the voter's true distance from the party and the perceived distance. As we have discussed earlier, the latter process involves non-rational decision processes. Party identifiers distort the positions of both their own party and the other parties so as to "explain" their vote and party sympathies better. Those who deviate from their party's position – such as leftist Conservatives – move their party closer to themselves, while they move the opposite party away from themselves. The fact that these two misperceptions tend to occur together suggests that they are something more than inaccurate perceptions. The information filter that causes inaccurate perceptions has all the appearance of deliberate selective perception.

One argument against using perceived position is therefore that it is an unnecessary complication if the aim is to explore a rational-choice model. In that case it is more fruitful to explore the causality of the models by studying electoral change:

> The purpose of the models is to link party strategy with popular support – to address the question: if a party takes a particular set of issue stands, what will happen to its public support? (Macdonald, Rabinowitz and Listhaug 1995, 460)

However, this theoretical position implies a throwing away of information that could be valuable. It seems to follow from it that voter judgments about the parties' issue positions would be superfluous if "external" in-

dicators of party positions, such as its parliamentary behaviour or campaign platform, were available. If, on the other hand, the "internal" indicators of voter judgments are allowed, why should it be permitted to use
the *mean* but not the *distribution* of these judgments? That distribution may
well have properties that might contribute to explaining electoral change
on the aggregate level. Suppose, for example, that one-half of the electors
think the Conservative position on a given issue has shifted to the right,
whereas the other half think it has shifted to the left. Then it would be
highly interesting to know the cause of these differences of perceptions, as
well as their effects on the election outcome.

Furthermore, misplacing a party may be a plausible reason for a particular group not to vote for it, and need not always be caused by identification
with a different party. Some left-wing voters may acquire a taste for voting
Conservative because they have distorted the Conservative position; but
others may have voted Conservative even though their perception of that
position is "correct". It might be worthwhile separating these two groups.

The directional theory should employ its full potential by asserting
that it is perceived positions, not "objective" positions, that evoke affect.
The further away from the center the party is believed to stand, the more
affect will it evoke. This proposition may be tested on one party at a time
because respondents differ in their perceptions of the party's stand. It
turns out to be strongly supported, as suggested by Table 4.5. Here, the
sample is subdivided by respondents' placement of the Conservative Party.
The correlation between issue position and Conservative support is observed to rise the more that party is placed to the right of the midpoint of
the scale (position 6).

Table 4.5. Issue position and Conservative support, by placement of the
Conservative Party (Britain, 1992).

Perceived posi-tion of the Con-servative Party	Correlation between:Cons. sympathyand issue position	N
1 to 5.75	0.19	(395)
6 to 6.75	0.43	(220)
7 to 7.75	0.56	(224)
8 to 8.75	0.67	(237)
9 to 9.75	0.73	(240)
10 to 11	0.73	(286)

The first row contains those respondents who placed the Conservative party left of center (though not necessarily left of the other parties). For these respondents the correlation is weak. This is not predicted by any of the two models; it suggests a category of uninformed and erratic voters who are anything but distance voters. Among the remaining voters the correlations rise the more extreme the placement of the Conservative party is to the right, until they reach a level of 0.73 among respondents who place the party at three or more positions right of center, that is, at positions 9-11.

Conclusion

The venerable proximity theory has a logic to it that makes it attractive, and it has led to fruitful advances as well in theory as in practical measurement. Without the concepts of party positions and utility, first developed by proximity theory, research on issue voting could not have reached its present stage. Proximity theory should not be rejected on the ground that it fails to predict the election outcome, or because many issues are not position issues. It was never intended to be a perfect model, only a working hypothesis particularly aimed at ideological issues.

However, there are two objections to proximity theory. One is that it postulates or at least implies a causal model in which voter positions are autonomous. This is highly unlikely, as we have witnessed in the foregoing chapter on party identification. The other objection comes from directional theory and claims that voter reactions to issues indicate affect rather than cognitive distances. This is in line with contemporary research in schema theory, as we shall se later. The directional theory has some defects, notably its failure to account for the attraction of center parties and its vagueness concerning the zone of responsibility, or penalty incurred for extremism; but it is consistent with the linear models that we have found to accord with much empirical experience.

Chapter 5
Issue Dimensions and Party Systems

Until now we have mainly dealt with issues and issue effects one at a time. But in a political culture characterized by heavy issue voting we must expect issues to cluster into broader issue dimensions. This is so both for logical and psychological reasons. The logic of political decision-making entails that one issue often has consequences for other issues. For example, a party that argues in favour of a more equal income distribution will be pressured toward explaining whether this should be done by means of controlling wages, by changing the tax system, by public works, or by extending social services. Hence, ends are logically related to means. But clustering also takes place for psychological reasons. It would be impossible for anybody except professional politicians and administrators to keep track of policy demands and proposals emerging from different sources in the political debate if one did not employ some simple way of mentally grouping them into a small number of groups.

But how many issue dimensions are there? The early Michigan studies (Converse 1964) found that "belief systems in mass publics" were weak except among a minority of ideological voters. Based on their findings one is inclined to put the number of dimensions close to zero. However, the American studies from the 1970s (for example, Nie with Andersen 1974) point toward at least one dominant dimension of the left-right character. This is more similar to the West European studies that took place in the same period. Going on to the 1980s, European researchers began to discern a second dimension, the so-called New Politics dimension (Baker, Dalton and Hildebrandt 1981). This was supposed to prevail among new generations of voters who were less committed than their predecessors to economic goals.

But all the time, some countries have exhibited older dimensions that interfered with the left-right dimension. Religious and moral issues, in particular, have constituted one separate dimension whereas language and ethnic issues have constituted another (Lijphart 1980). Some researchers have seen these as issues carried over from the pre-industrial phase, whereas the economic left-right dimension has grown up under the impact of industrialization. In post-industrial society, then, new issues such as minority rights and environmental protection are added on top of the left-right issues.

A basic question is, however, to what extent these intersecting dimensions are bound together by a common left-right schema. This is suggested by a theory that will be discussed first. After that we shall examine the differentiation of issues into two or more dimensions and the content of these dimensions, drawing on material from the British and Danish elections studies. This includes an evaluation of the New Politics paradigm.

The Left-Right Schema

For the last two hundred years the concepts of the political left and right have been part of the European political tradition. They have been employed to label parties and movements, as well as their issue positions and political goals or "causes", and politically conscious voters have identified themselves and their opponents by these labels or by labeling themselves "centrist". The left-right scale has become the most widely known and used schema in European politics, at least on the continent.

Psychological research has shed some light on the conditions for the use of cognitive schemas. Conover and Feldman (1984) cite social psychological research suggesting that schemas are cognitive structures used by the individual to store and order information which the individual later retrieves in order to perceive new objects and making decision about a course of action. In order to serve these functions the schema should have "a pyramidal structure, hierarchically organized with more abstract or general information at the top and categories of more specific information nested within the general categories" (Taylor and Crocker 1981, 92 quoted in Conover and Feldman 1984, 97).

There is no requirement as to the content of a schema, or what will be at the top of the pyramid. But the labels of left and right fit the description well. The general use of these labels suggests that they have a very abstract quality and will tend to express the main conflict in the political system. Since the main conflict may move from one issue to another, the "meaning" or content of left and right may change, and it may differ somewhat from one party system to another. Obviously, the labels of left and right are mental tools for the ordering of a large number of cognitive and affective objects into a simpler form, and for referring to such objects in the political discourse. Thus they serve the functions of orientation for the individual participant and of communication in the political collective.

Thus, a scheme is more than a summary of the issues that are correlated with it. Left and right may be used to order parties or other actors (such as political movements and interest groups) without the use of issues. It is quite possible for an observer to acquire a feeling for left and right simply by looking at how often a party enters into coalitions and conflicts with other parties in the parliament. In fact this is what researchers do when they apply multidimensional scaling to legislative roll calls. It is also possible to order parties from left to right merely on the basis of sympathy shown for the parties. The more persons who like one party tend to like another party too, the closer these two parties are assumed to be. This is done in multidimensional scaling of party sympathies (e.g. Nannestad 1989, and Rusk and borre 1974, in the case of Danish parties). Such procedures are issue-free, and the relative stability of the patterns that are often found illustrates that the left/right nature of party competition may work in its own right across a shifting number of issues.

Left-Right Self-Placement

In the early 1970s, surveys in a number of European countries began to include questions about how the respondent would place himself or herself on a left-right scale consisting of about ten positions. The scale was included in the Eurobarometer surveys and so made possible a comparison of a number of European electorates. A comparative study (Inglehart and Klingemann 1976) suggested that political parties were the most important connotation, but that issue orientations and orientations to groups such as "working class" or "church-goers" were often also indicated when respondents explained what they understood by left and right. It is even possible that left, right, and center may become labels for voter groups with which the voters can identify. Such a group may have some degree of we-feeling and a common animosity toward the other groups. But they do not necessarily fall on a scale; left-wingers may, for example, be just as much opposed to centrists as to right-wingers.

This discussion leads to a "schema hypothesis" which states that left and right self-placements are indicators of general political reference groups whose partisan choice and issue positions may vary. We may illustrate this hypothesis with Danish data, but not British. The British tradition, argued in Butler and Stokes (1969) is that left and right are very little used, and where used, have no unambiguous content; in the British election surveys, the respondents are consequently not asked to place themselves on the scale. However, in the Danish surveys the scale has been used since 1979, and the results are cumulating.

First, the theory that left and right constitute long-term bases of voter identification seems to imply that the sizes of these groups are not susceptible to short-term change. This is not true in the case of Denmark. Table 5.1 shows evidence of a quite lively change during the period 1979-94, for which the left-right position has been measured.

Between 1981 and 1984 public opinion swung toward the right; then, between 1984 and 1987 there was a strong reaction, with public opinion swinging toward the left. Finally, the period from 1987 to 1994 has witnessed another rightward shift, making 1994 the year with the largest majority of voters on the right since the measurement began. These changes in the public mood are inconsistent with the notion that left and right are basic long-term voter identifications.

Second, schema theory implies that the issue content of left and right should vary over time. Also on this point the evidence is negative. Left-right placement in Denmark is permanently correlated with a set of traditional economic issues. The distribution of left-right positions that we saw in Table 5.1 rather closely follows an index of these issues, as Table 5.2 shows.

Comparing these figures with those in Table 5.1 for the five elections in which they were both measured, we observe that they are very equal in all years: in 1979 (-8 and –9), in 1984 (-15 and –17), in 1987 (+9 and +11), in 1990 (-12 and –10), and in 1994 (both –19). Hence, in the aggregated data the index conveys the same information as does the left-right distribution.

Table 5.1. Distribution of voters by left-right self-placement in Denmark 1979-94.

	1979	1981	1984	1987	1990	1994
Left (position 1-4)	22%	25%	21%	30%	25%	21%
Center (5-6)	48	45	43	49	38	39
Right (7-10)	30	30	36	21	37	40
Left-Right difference	-8%	-5%	-15%	9%	-12%	-19%

Table 5.2. Distribution of voters by an index of five issue positions in Denmark 1979-94.

	1979	1984	1987	1988	1990	1994
Leftist attitudes	29%	25%	38%	35%	25%	20%
Centrist attitudes	33	33	35	34	40	41
Rightist attitudes	38	42	27	31	35	39
Left-Right difference	-9%	-17%	11%	4%	-10%	-19%

Note. Leftist attitudes are defined as scores 4-6, centrist as scores 7-9, and rightist as scores 10-12 on an additive index of responses to four issues: on social reforms, on income redistribution, on state control of private business, and on nationalization of banks and big industries (for precise wordings, see Borre and Goul Andersen 1997, 29).

The evidence is that the issue content has not changed over these fifteen years. These data suggest that left-right self-placement operates as a sort of super-issue indexing a core of conflict-producing issues.

Third, according to schema theory left-right self-placement should convey information not only on issue positions but also on party preference. At this point one is apt to agree with the theory. In accounting for the individual vote, left-right position is a better predictor and tends to overshadow the issue positions. For example, in the Danish 1994 survey the socialist/bourgeois vote is correlated with the voter's left-right self-placement with an r=0.66 but with the issue index with only r=0.49. The result is that when an issue voting model of the socialist or bourgeois vote, using these four issues, is controlled for left-right position, the issue effects are drastically reduced.

The inference is that left-right self-placement means at least two things: (1) issue preference on a set of classical economic issues, and (2) party preference or party identification. The latter connotation means that we should not control for left-right self-placement in assessing issue effects on the vote or party sympathies. That would be double counting. Left-right self-placement should not be allowed it to oust meaningful and self-explanatory issues from a model of issue voting.

The conclusion that left and right are also attached to parties does not mean, however, that these labels may easily be confused with the names of the parties. Several Danish parties carry the labels of left and right in their names; notably the largest bourgeois party calls itself "Venstre", or "Left". But this has not prevented survey respondents from placing it on the right, and even moving it further toward the right between 1979 and 1994, consistent with the judgment of informed observers. Similar examples are reported for other countries (for Scandinavia, see Gilljam and Oscarsson 1996).

Value Dimensions

The hypothesis of a single, or at least over-riding, issue dimension on which both voters and parties polarize is consistent with the Marxist theory of industrial society. In that theory, the material issues of economic equality and property ownership constituted the dominant issues. The underlying force producing a polarization on these issues was, of course, the class war between the working class and the bourgeoisie. The issue positions of other classes were ambiguous: for example, the intellectuals might side with the workers, and the petty bourgeoisie including the farmers might contribute with ideas carried over from an earlier and declining social order. Hence the party system and dominant issue dimension might not concretely reflect the class interest: both were contaminated by ideological perceptions.

The hypothesis of an all-pervasive material dimension was undermined by Max Weber in his insistence that ideas about the nation-state, religion, science and technology were likely to find political expression in non-material issue positions. He saw political movements as influenced by "value-rationality" rather than by objective material interest. Later, we shall discuss this point in connection with the self-interest hypothesis of policy attitudes.

Thus, when empirical research in political attitudes began after World War II, it was looking for a variety of value dimensions to explain when and why political issues emerged, and which positions would be taken on these issues by different population groups. A strong impetus came from social psychology. During the 1950s the attention was drawn to authoritarian issues and their capacity for crosscutting the left-right dimension (Adorno et al. 1950; Eysenck 1954; Lipset 1960). Issues of law and order, of minority rights and racial equality, and of democratic liberties, were observed to rise to prominence in certain elections and to form the backbone of mass movements.

In the early 1970s the American psychologist Milton Rokeach, in *The Nature of Human Values*, showed that people's preference order between a set of 18 goals or 'terminal values' was surprisingly stable. While most of his selection of values dealt with religious values or values of personal accomplishment, two were especially important for the person's political choice, namely, freedom and equality. Those ranking freedom high were generally adherents of democratic parties whereas those ranking this value low tended to have sympathies for communist or fascist parties. The ranking of equality went across this divide. Those high on equality would prefer either a socialist or communist party, while those ranking it low would prefer a capitalist or fascist party. Therefore, the combined ranking of these two values indicated a choice among four ideologies and impinged upon a number of issues.

Rokeach's theory anticipates the *permanency* of values. This may not have been the most relevant message to bring to political science in the early 1970s. More in line with the tide in politics and public opinion was the theory of value change that Ronald Inglehart launched in 1971. In an attempt to account for the "youth rebellion" and to forecast its long-range political consequences, Inglehart suggested that a new set of "postmaterialist" values (originally termed "postbourgeois"), installed in the new generations of voters, were slowly replacing the "materialist" values around which the political conflicts had traditionally rotated.

Values are beliefs about what is desirable. They are hypothesized to be more stable and deep-seated than attitudes to issues, and they do not relate to behaviour as directly as attitudes do. However, values are likely to differ from one generation to the next because of experiences from war, economic crises, and changes in the family pattern. Hence, in the long run values might change the political agenda of economically advanced nations as new generations gradually replace the old.

In the approach of Rokeach and Inglehart, values are measured directly by asking respondents to rank various desirable states of society or individuals by their importance. The anthology, *The Impact of Values* (van Deth and Scarbrough 1995) distinguish between religious values, material left-right values, and postmaterial values. It sets out to show how these value dimensions affect a multitude of attitudes to societal objects.

New Politics

Inglehart's theory of value change, in combination with the left-right conception of politics, has given rise to a theory of *New Politics*. According to the proponents of that theory (Dalton and Hildebrandt 1978; Baker,

Dalton, and Hildebrandt 1981; Knutsen 1985; Flanagan 1987; Dalton 1988; Müller-Rommel 1990; Jenssen 1993; Borre 1995; Borre and Goul Andersen 1997), the political agenda of economically advanced ("postindustrial") countries will gradually change. A traditional preoccupation with physical and material security will be replaced by a concern for quality-of-life issues such as the environment, minority rights and equal treatment, protection of democratic norms of participation, and a more rational view of moral issues.

This will not make the left-right schema obsolete, but it will extend the specter of left and right to include a non-material New Left along with the material Old Left, and a non-material New Right in addition to the material Old Right. In contrast to the old politics cleavage, which was based mainly on social class, the new politics cleavage will be based primarily on educational level, since the capacity for information processing is the most valued resource in the postindustrial society.

On the New Politics dimension, people with high education will place themselves on the left, whereas those with low education will be on the right. Consequently the emergence of the new dimension can be expected to cause splits in both of the traditional party camps. When new politics issues are made topical in an election, workers will move toward the right because of their lack of education, while educated sectors of the middle class will move toward the left.

These splits may give rise to new parties, depending on the force of the new issues and the ease of entry into the party system. The parties of the New Left and the New Right will combine members of previously antagonistic population classes. On the whole, the party systems of Western political systems will tend toward a structure with two issue dimensions rather than one left-right dimension. The establishment of the new politics dimension will give rise to a period of instability, the new issues accounting for most of the issue voting.

Such is the string of hypotheses that can be derived from the New Politics perspective. New Politics theory seeks to bridge the gap between values and voting, and according to that theory, values should emerge in the form of issue dimensions – either as a structure of political agendas or as a structure of positions on issues. The New Politics theory appears at first glance to provide a promising explanation for the breakthrough of the new left and the green parties in the 1970s and 1980s in many systems, and the subsequent breakthrough of the anti-immigration parties of the new right in the second half of the 1980s.

Criticism of the New Politics Paradigm

However, there are also grounds for not relying too much on the weight of this sketchy evidence. In the first place, material issues such as unemployment, welfare services, and the tax level, have continued to be the main fuel for partisan struggle during the last decade in many European countries.

Another criticism is that even if material or economic issues may lose in importance relative to non-economic issues, it may be questioned to what extent non-material issues as far apart as environmental protection, women's rights, and aid to developing countries will ever combine to form a unified dimension. In a political world increasingly post-structuralist, they are likely to remain a scattered set of issues with a potential for occasionally upsetting the partisan balance. This seems to be the position favoured by, for example, Swedish and Norwegian researchers (Giljam and Holmberg 1993, Aardal and Valen 1989, Jenssen 1993).

It has also been argued that the traditional old politics dimension is really two dimensions, one that concerns economic security and another that concerns physical security (either external, *i.e.,* defence issues, or internal, *i.e.,* law and order issues). According to Flanagan (1987), physical security mixes with economic security in Inglehart's battery so as to confound the materialist-postmaterialist value dimension. A recent comparative study of political agendas (Roller 1995) found these two agendas to be practically uncorrelated. It may be added that religious and moral issues constitute another non-material conflict dimension of long standing in European politics; in the New Politics scheme the place of these values is uncertain, and for example, Norwegian politics shows that religious voters are not always found among the new right.

Third, new politics theory leaves room for different hypotheses as to how the new values become expressed in the party system. In general, values theory tends to regard the party system as being "frozen" along the lines of traditional issues (cf. Lipset and Rokkan 1967), and therefore as reacting only with some reluctance and delay to the new values and value change among the electorate.

Factor Analysis of Issue Dimensions

Factor analysis of issue orientations has become the standard way of discerning issue dimensions. In the most common research strategy, one or a few latent issue dimensions (which may or may not correspond to values) are identified by means of factor analysis. When issues are scaled by means of factor analysis, responses to issues are assumed to be affected by one or several factors, which may be uncorrelated with each other ("orthogonal") or correlated. The output of a factor analysis informs us (1) whether the variables fall into one, two or more factors, (2) the correlations, or loadings, of the variables on each factor, (3) the amount of variance explained by each factor, which can also be measured as eigenvalues of the factor, and (4) the positions, or scores, of each observation on these factors. However, care should be taken because the factors one finds depend very much on the variables that one has entered in the analysis. In many cases, adding or removing an issue will change the factors, or issue dimensions, that result from the analysis.

Factor analyses has confirmed that in many West European countries, the New Politics dimension seems to play a marginal role; this is the case in, for example, Britain and Sweden. In a comparative study it was found that issue positions on eight budget items clustered in three dimensions: (1) a "welfare" dimension containing demands concerned with old age pensions, health service, unemployment benefits, and education – (2) a "beauty" dimension concerned with expenditures for culture and arts, and environmental protection – and (3) an "order" dimension concerned with expenditures for law enforcement and defence (Huseby 1995; Borre 1995). While the "beauty" dimension was positively correlated with postmaterial values, and the "order" dimension negatively so, the "welfare" dimension, by far the most important both for the voter's party preference and attitude to the political system, was uncorrelated with postmaterial values but correlated with traditional left-right values.

New Politics and the Party System

The first test of the New Politics hypothesis must consist in evidence that the structure of issue positions is two-dimensional. If that is the case, the second test is evidence that the party system represents both of these dimensions. If we think of the voters as taking policy stands in a two-dimensional issue space, corresponding to the Old and New Politics dimension, we may distinguish three possible outcomes:

(1) None of the existing parties react to the new values that occupy their voters, and although there are ample differences in issue positions among the voters, these differences cannot be translated into a partisan choice; they may, however, lead to internal fractions within the parties.

(2) The existing parties distinguish themselves in their stands on the

new issues, and in that case, there will be a mixture of issue voting on the old and the new issues.

(3) The old parties will continue to represent the old issues but new parties will be formed to represent the new issues.

In the first reports on new politics issues, the second option prevailed. For the United States, Miller and Levitin (1976) found that Democratic voters had differentiated themselves from Republican voters on the new issues of race equality, urban riots, campus unrest, marijuana, sexual minorities and so forth. For Germany, Hildebrandt and Dalton (1978) found a similar difference emerging between the Social Democractic voters and the Christian Democratic or Christian Social voters. Of course, Germany was later to approach the third option with the formation of the Green party in 1980 and the Republican anti-immigration party later in the 1980s.

More lively multiparty systems often feature a struggle among minor parties in their pursuit to seize particular issues in order to acquire an image that distinguishes a specific party from other parties. This tendency shows up when issues are cross-classified with other issues in what is often termed a *policy space*: small parties are seen to deviate from the rest so as to fill out the corners of a two-dimensional policy space. In accounts of election surveys from multiparty systems, the conventional way to represent these possibilities takes the form of graphing the parties, and the voters of the parties, in a two-dimensional space. To the extent that the parties are seen to spread out over the entire issue space, the axes of that space may be argued to represent a value space. Thus for Sweden, Holmberg (1981, 193) found a second dimension representing the issue of nuclear power. For Norway, Valen (1981, 231) found a tendency that industrial growth versus environmental protection formed a second dimension and the abortion issue (together with religious and moralistic values), a third dimension in the party system.

Issue Dimensions in Denmark

According to the Rokeach freedom/equality scheme as well as the Inglehart materialist/postmaterialist scheme, one would expect issue positions to fall into two dimensions. Accordingly, the first problem is whether the responses to issue items really are two-dimensional. If so, it may be meaningful to study the voters of different parties as they assume different positions in a two-dimensional issue space with the axes V_O and V_N, where V_O represents the Old Politics dimension and V_N, the New Politics dimension.

In the case of the Danish data, a two-dimensional pattern indeed emerged in the 1990 and 1994 elections (Borre 1995; Borre and Goul Andersen 1997). One factor was the economic left-right, as measured by positions on four issues: social reforms, economic equality, state control of business, and wage increases. The other factor was a non-economic left-right as measured by positions on aid to developing nations, treatment of violent crimes, environmental protection, and immigration policy (Borre and Goul Andersen 1997, 43). Scores on the latter, but not the former factor, were correlated with the Inglehart battery of four value items (*ibid.*, 51).

The first hypothesis of a two-dimensional structure of issue orientations was thus borne out by the Danish 1990 and 1994 surveys. The second hypothesis, dealing with an educational polarization on the new politics dimension, similar to the social class cleavage on the old politics dimension, was also supported. Dividing the 1990 respondents into the new left and the new right depending on their scores on the four new politics issues, we found that the size of the new left varied from 16 percent among those with 7 years or less schooling, to 64 percent among those with 12 or more years of schooling. In 1994, the corresponding figures were 20 and 68 percent.

The third hypothesis is that elections, increasingly, will be decided by New Politics rather than Old Politics issues. The simplest way to test that hypothesis would be to divide the respondents into four groups by cross-tabulating their scores on the new and the old politics issues. This is done in Table 5.3.

We observe in the left-hand section of the table that the parties which were in government in the 1994 election received their highest support (57 percent) from the new right / old left group, or what might be called the

Table 5.3. 1990 and 1994 vote for the Danish Social Democrat-center government, by ideological group, and the size of the ideological groups.

| | | Government Vote | | Size of Ideological Group | |
		Old Left	Old Right	Old Left	Old Right
New Right	1994	57	25	30	30
New Left	1994	53	36	26	14
New Right	1990	69	33	34	27
New Left	1990	54	35	27	12

"authoritarian left". Slightly less support (53 percent) was given it by the new left / old left group, or "left wing", which can be explained by the fact that the government excluded the left-wing parties. Less support (36 percent) came from the new left / old right group, which might be termed the "green bourgeois" voters. The least support (25 percent) came from the new right / old right group, or "right wing", where the bourgeois opposition was concentrated.

The right-hand half of the table indicates the size of these four groups in 1990 and 1994. These figures did not change much between the two elections; still, the old right groups together increased their size by 5 percentage points at the cost of the old left. Thus, a moderate rightward shift on economic issues was noted.

The table contains in a compressed form the information relevant for an assessment of the new politics model of electoral change. Although the government had managed the economic issues well since its takeover in early 1993, it stood to lose anyway because of right-wing sentiments on non-economic issues, especially the refugee issue and the law and order issue. This hypothesis is clearly corroborated by the data in the table. The government lost 8-12 percent of the vote in the two new-right groups, but nothing among the new left. Hence we may conclude that issue effects on new politics issues rather than old politics issues were indeed decisive in the Danish 1994 election.

Issue Dimensions in Britain

In British data we may argue in favour of at least partial corroboration of the New Politics thesis. Heath et al. (1991, 174) found a two-factor solution for 1987. The first factor included the issues of nationalization, extending social welfare and the national health service, and redistributing wealth and income. The second factor contained attitudes to the death penalty, punishment of crime, equal opportunities for blacks and Asians, and aid to poorer countries. Items on abortion and pornography loaded weakly on this factor. In exploring the "green" dimension in a separate analysis they found (p.188) that the nuclear power issue and the issue of protecting the countryside formed two separate dimensions.

McAllister and Mughan (1985, 1987) in their studies of the elections between 1974 and 1983, found four factors: (1) socialism, (2) ethnocentrism, or racism, (3) permissiveness, or traditional morality, and (4) social welfare. They explicitly exclude the issue of nuclear defence as being relevant only in 1983. Whereas the first and fourth factor mainly belong in the Old Politics dimension, the second factor is reminiscent of New Politics.

In tracing a number of issues through the four elections from October 1974 to 1992, we found that the same *three* factors emerged in every election. The first was an economic left-right factor, corresponding to Rokeach's equality value. It accounted for between 25 and 22 percent of the variance of responses over eleven issues, and contained six items about (1) redistributing income and wealth in favor of ordinary working people, (2) spending more money to get rid of domestic poverty, (3) extending or restricting welfare benefits, (4) cutting either taxes or health and social services, (5) giving workers more say in the running of their workplace, besides (6) the nationalization or privatization issue referred to above.

The second factor, accounting for between 13 and 11 percent of the variance, was a morality factor containing two issues about (1) the right to show nudity and sex in films and magazines, and (2) the availability of abortion on the national health service. The third factor, accounting for 11 or 10 percent of the variance, was a racial attitude factor with two items, (1) equality for colored people and (2) aid to poorer countries in Africa and Asia. However, in 1987 and 1992 the third factor also contains items about pulling out the troops in Northern Ireland and about efforts to ensure equality for women; thus it is a more general attitude toward minorities.

These findings are consistent with those of McAllister and Mughan, as their social welfare factor may, with their socialism factor, easily integrate into our equality factor when the choice of items to enter the analysis is slightly different. Thus, regarding the *content* of the factors, there is some support for the values theories of Rokeach and Inglehart. Regarding the *number* of factors, both theories seem to go too far in assuming two-dimensionality. Finally, regarding the *development* over time, Rokeach predicts a stable pattern, whereas Inglehart predicts the second dimension to gradually gain momentum over the years. On this point, Rokeach seems more correct, as there is little indication of a systematic value change in the British factor analyses.

But New Politics theory also predicts that the non-material dimensions will differentiate between the parties. This is much harder to confirm in the British case. As in the Danish 1990-94 elections, we shall analyze the British 1987-92 elections by dividing the samples into fourfold tables, one for each election, with old and new politics scores as the axes. For an index of old politics, we use the following four items:

Income and wealth should be redistributed towards ordinary working people (Question 38b in 1987, 47a in 1992)

Are you generally in favour of more nationalization of companies by government, more privatization of companies by government, or should things be left as they are now? (Question 36a in 1987, 45a in 1992)

The welfare benefits that are available today have (1) gone much too far, (2) gone too far, (3) about right, (4) not gone far enough, or (5) not gone nearly far enough (Question 43a in 1987, 50a in 1992).

Do you think the government should or should not spend more money to get rid of poverty? (Question 33b in 1987, 44b in 1992)

For an index of new politics, we use another set of four items:

The government should give more aid to poor countries in Africa and Asia (Question 38d in 1987, 47b in 1992)

Attempts to give equal opportunities to women in Britain have (1) gone much too far, (2) gone too far, (3) about right, (4) not gone far enough, or (5) not gone nearly far enough (Question 43b in 1987, 50b in 1992)

Attempts to give equal opportunities to black people and Asians in Britain have (1) gone much too far, (2) gone too far, (3) about right, (4) not gone far enough, or (5) not gone nearly far enough (Question 43f n 1987, 50e in 1992)

Do you think the government should or should not pull British troops out of Northern Ireland immediately? (Question 26a in 1987, 31a in 1992)

The responses to each item were coded from 1 (left) to 5 (right) – in the case of the nationalization/privatization item, which had only three positions, these were coded 1, 3, and 5 – and added up to an index for old politics position and one for new politics position. These indices were then collapsed into two groups of approximately equal size. Table 5.4 shows the Conservative vote in 1987 and 1992 for each of the four groups of respondents.

The left half of the table indicates that the Conservative vote depends much more on the material issues, or old politics issues, than on the non-material or new politics issues. The difference between the columns is around 50 percentage points, whereas the difference between the rows is only around 10 percentage points. The change between the two elections took the form of a Conservative progress in all four corners of the table, the difference between the ideological groups being very small, between 4 and 7 percent.

Table 5.4. 1987 and 1992 vote for the British Conservatives, by ideological group, and the size of these groups.

		Conservative vote		Size of Ideological Group	
		Old Left	Old Right	Old Left	Old Right
New Right	1987	23%	76%	19%	31%
	1992	30	82	23	26
New Left	1987	13%	64%	31%	19%
	1992	19	69	37	14

However, the Conservatives did not have progress in the 1992 election in the aggregate: in the sample, the party got 46 percent of the vote in both surveys. How was this possible when the party had progress in all four corners of the table? This is clarified in the right-hand side of the table. Here, it turns out that the New Right / Old Left group grew from 19 to 23 percent, and the New Left / Old Left group, from 31 to 37 percent. Consequently there was a leftward shift in the attitudes of old politics from 50 to 60 percent leftist over the five years. The Conservatives succeeded in maintaining their strength in the 1992 election because they compensated for an adverse shift in issue attitudes by increasing their support both among the left and right.

The two elections, the Danish 1994 election and the British 1992 election, exhibit very different types of change. While the Danish election shows a loss of support for a moderate left government due to its failure to placate the new right, the British election shows a Conservative government capable of maintaining its strength in the face of leftward shifts in the attitudes of old politics. As for new politics theory, none of the two elections exhibit a shift on non-economic issue orientation, while both exhibit a shift on economic issue orientations – a major shift to the left in Britain, and a minor shift to the right in Denmark. In both cases the governments were able to fence off the damaging consequences of that shift. The Danish government, however, seemed to have been too "postmaterial" for the bulk of the population, and to have been punished for such an ideology.

Chapter 6
Issue Priority

In Chapters 2-5 we have been studying position models. Common to these models is that the voter's goal has been compared to the policy goal of the party, and the correspondence or agreement between the two has been hypothesized to increase the voter's positive attitude toward the party. But, as we noted in connection with the consistency model in Chapter 1, there are other ways of attaining consistency. These apply to position issues as well but they become particularly relevant when we move away from position issues and toward policy areas where there is a general consensus about which goals should be pursued.

Valence issues, as defined by Donald Stokes (1963), are issues on which everybody shares the same position. Every voter wants economic growth, a high level of employment, low inflation, law and order, peace, and a healthy and beautiful environment. All governments and parties want to be associated with these goals. Valence issues therefore do not provide the voter with an opportunity to assess his or her spatial distance to various parties as a basis for preferring one of them to the others. The choice must be made on other criteria, such as:

(1)   How important is the political goal or problem?
(2)   Can the party or government be trusted to handle the problem seriously and competently?
(3)   Has the government handled the problem successfully during the period of its rule?
(4)   Has society developed in a positive or negative direction lately?

These criteria lead to issue voting models that attempt to measure issue priority (types 4-6 in our typology in Table 1.1) and government performance (types 7-10). Issue priority will be explored in the present chapter, whereas the performance model will be discussed in Chapter 7.

All experience tells us that valence issues are extremely important in affecting the outcomes of elections. A major part of the campaign debate deals with questions about which problems should be at the top of the political agenda. In addition, questions about the government's record in solving the political problems and improving the citizens' situation are fixed ingredients in any campaign. Also questions of what the opposition could have done better in one policy area or another is often raised. In addition, many of those issues, which we have treated as positional, may really be valence issues. As we have seen in the foregoing chapter, those political values that underlie issue positions are often about priorities, rather than opposed to another. In brief, modern elections may turn out to be less concerned with divisive issues than consensus issues, but this does not necessarily mean that issue voting is becoming less important.

In the case of the salience model, we are dealing with issue orientations for which the logic of issue position and issue proximity still applies. One can think of a voter and a party as choosing their positions on a dimension from "very important problem" to "not at all important". Or one may think of respondents and parties as placed on a continuum from "fighting inflation is more important" to "fighting unemployment is more important". In the case of performance, this logic no longer applies. One cannot think of a voter or a party as preferring the position "the problem should be handled poorly" to the position "should be handled well". Issue priorities therefore may be treated almost in the same way as issue positions. However, being valence issues, they do not advocate a certain policy.

Measuring Issue Priority

Looking back at the struggle between socialist, liberal, and conservative movements and parties, it was probably always the case that the reformists fought not only for particular issue positions; they also fought simply to be heard and taken seriously. The struggle was a struggle about the political agenda as much as it was a struggle for particular ideological ideas or practical bills of reform.

But the theory of voting has been fairly slow to integrate the importance or salience of issues into its conceptual framework. The Elmira study of the 1948 election, conducted by the Columbia scholars, observed that even though voters of the two parties might differ in their positions on issues, they tended to agree on which issues were important. This was consistent with the "value consensus" concept favoured by the leading sociological school of thought, the functional theory (Berelson, Lazarsfeld, and McPhee 1954).

If all parties and/or all major voter groups agree on which issues are the most important, the priority of issues of course cannot serve as a criterion for choosing among the parties. There must be differences among the parties as well as among the voters before we can speak of higher or lower degrees of consistency between voters and parties. A particularly high degree of consistency can be said to exist when both the voter and the party emphasize the same issue. A voter is attracted to a party that has the same political agenda as he himself.

The Michigan researchers did not confine themselves to the study of position issues. In fact Stokes (1963), as we have seen in a foregoing chapter, criticized the spatial theory for dealing with position issues only. Converse, in his belief systems article, pointed toward the existence of various "issue publics" as one of the factors that prevented the electorate from manifesting a single coherent attitude toward issues (Converse 1964). And the normal vote model, discussed in Chapter 3, works equally well or poorly on valence issues and position issues.

Therefore, the problem is how to measure issue priority and how to integrate this dimension with the spatial model so as to construct a more complete model of issue voting.

The salience of issues for individual voters may be measured by questions such as "which political problems do you think are the most important for politicians to solve?" Sometimes these questions are asked in the beginning of the survey and involve open-ended responses that are coded at a later stage; sometimes the interviewer consults a list of problems and codes the responses on location; and sometimes the respondent is asked to choose from a list of problems. In either case we may divide the respondents into groups with different issue priorities.

In addition, some surveys use follow-up questions on issue positions so as to ask, "Do you think this issue is very important, somewhat important, or not at all important?" By making use of the responses to these items, it is possible in practice to observe whether the correlation produced by the position model is higher among those who think the issue is important than among those who think it is unimportant.

A research strategy that saves survey time is to combine issue position and issue salience into the same item. Respondents may be asked to react to a series of proposals on a scale from "very important to do" to "very important not to do" whatever the proposals say. This method is used extensively in, for example, Swedish and British surveys. From such a question one can disentangle the directional and the salience component of the issue orientation from one another by comparing the extreme stands with the more moderate stands on the same side of the issue.

Issue priority, or salience, is also translated into positions when respondents are asked to choose among two supposedly opposite goals according to their priority. For example, the goal of economic growth may be confronted with the goal of environmental protection. A particularly common type is the "trade-off" item asking the respondent whether it is more important to fight unemployment than to fight inflation, or whether it is better to reduce income taxes than to extend welfare services and redistribution. Thus, position issues may be valence issues in disguise.

Combining Salience and Position

In order to analyze the effect of issue priority, when we are dealing with position issues, one research strategy is to treat the salience of the issue as a weight factor in the proximity model, or to filter out non-salient issues. The latter strategy was followed in an empirical analysis by RePass (1971), in which he called attention to the effect of saliency factors upon the issue effects estimated in the 1960 and 1964 American elections. He argued that "salient issues had almost as much weight as party identification in predicting voting choice" (RePass 1971, 400). Though this lay in direct extension of Converse's notion of issue publics, the effect was to undermine the Michigan position, because the implication was that issue voting only *seemed* low because researchers have required their respondents to have opinions on precisely those issues which the researchers pronounce to be important in a given election. When the respondents themselves are given a choice among issues, they are able to come up with consistent attitudes.

Against this view, others have argued that the respondents seem to take their information on what is important from the media or the politicians rather than from themselves, a finding which agrees with the studies of agenda-setting in communications research. There is a suspicion that many voters have almost no idea of which issues have influenced their vote. As put by Rivers (1988, 738):

> Unfortunately, people are notoriously bad reporters of their own decision processes. The Gallup Poll, for example, periodically asks its respondents what they think is the most important problem facing the country. While this series fairly accurately mirrors what is in the newspapers at any given time, it does not seem to be very closely related to the factors which influence individual voting.

In testing the model, it seems more accurate to study variations in salience rather than merely discarding non-salient issues, such as RePass does. For an example we may use the British nationalization versus privatization issue. Besides differentiating the respondents along an 11 points scale, which we may code as running from –5 (nationalization) to +5 (privatization), a follow-up question differentiated them on a four point scale depending on whether the respondent thought the issue had been "extremely important", "very important", "not very important", or "not important at all" for the voting choice. The more important the issue is, the stronger the tendency toward consistency between the issue position and the vote. For a test, the 1992 correlations between issue position and Conservative, resp. Labour, voting within these four categories were as follows:

For both parties, the strength of the correlation rises steadily with the perceived importance of the issue. It may be added that such is the case with three other issues questioned in the same survey.

Hence, including a term of interaction between respondent's issue position and the importance attached to the issue is warranted. The salience of an issue may be hypothesized to operate as a weight factor that should be attached to the individual's party preference model when issue positions are employed to predict the vote:

$$\text{Vote} = a + b * \text{Issue Salience} * \text{Issue Position}$$

This expresses the hypothesis that for issues with low salience, the voter's issue position has little impact on the probability of voting for the party,

Table 6.1. Correlations between vote and issue position, by perceived importance of the issue. British 1992 election.

Nationalization *vs* Privatization is:	Correlation		
	Con. vote with issue position	Lab. vote with issue position	(N)
Extremely important	0.63	-0.47	(154)
Very important	0.44	-0.42	(471)
Not very important	0.31	-0.29	(610)
Not important at all	0.12	-0.13	(159)

while for salient issues, the vote is strongly dependent on the issue position. As an example we may look at the vote for the Danish rightwing parties in the 1998 election in connection with the issue of how many refugees Denmark should accept. For the purpose of Table 6.2 the voter's position on that issue was coded: 2=far fewer, 1=fewer, and 0=as now or more than now. The salience of the issue was gauged by a question about the importance of issues about refugees and immigrants when the respondent chose a party. For the present purpose the responses were coded 2=decisive importance, 1=great importance and 0=some, less, or no importance.

If we include both position and importance, as well as the product of the two, in the regression model, the result is as follows:

Rightwing vote = .01 + .090 Position*Importance + .008 Position – .002 Importance.

The only significant coefficient is that of the interaction term Position*Importance. Since the value of this product runs from 0 to 4, its coefficient of 0.09 predicts the rightwing vote to vary from 0 to 36 percent in the table. The correlation between the vote and this interaction term alone is r=0.43. If we had relied on the position item alone we would not have obtained a correlation higher than r=0.33; if we had relied on the salience item, a correlation no higher than r=0.29. It is their combination that produces the good fit.

Table 6.2. Danish right-wing vote 1998, in percent. By position on, and importance of, the refugee issue.

| | Importance of Issue | | |
Position	Decisive	Great	Less
Take far fewer refugees	42% (217)	12% (117)	11% (71)
Fewer than now	16% (125)	6% (207)	3% (272)
As now, or more than now	4% (135)	1% (263)	1% (374)

Note. Numbers in parentheses = 100 percent.

Trading Off Valence Issues

Next, let us take a brief look at those survey items that are not really position issues but disguised pairs of valence issues. An example is the unemployment versus inflation item, which is traditionally asked in the British election surveys. Testing it on the British 1992 data, moderately strong issue effects were found. The item differentiated between 11 positions, from –5=Getting people back to work should be the government's top priority, to +5=Keeping prices down should be the government's top priority. The Conservative vote was found to rise by 3.6% for each step, and the Labour vote, to fall by 3.1%. The correlation between issue position and the vote was 0.21 in the case of the Conservative vote and 0.19 in the case of the Labour vote.

In general it improves the analysis when respondents are forced into making a choice, such as is done in regular position items. However, there is a drawback to relying too much on this type of questioning, because either the voters or the parties do not see the issue in this light. And they may have good reasons for keeping them apart. Trade-off items may create a false dichotomy by forcing respondents to choose between political objectives that do not exclude one another. For example, this may well be the case with items that ask the respondents to choose between industrial growth and environmental protection. If instead the two objective were rated for their importance by the same respondents, it is quite possible that the rating of these two objectives would turn out not to be inversely correlated.

The Salience Model

Establishing the importance of an issue to the voter is only one side of the coin, the other side is the importance of the issue to the parties. As we noted above, a voter cannot make use of his or her assessment of the salience of an issue in choosing between the parties unless the party itself has a stand on the issue that singles it out from other parties. The effect of the salience of an issue therefore must hinge on the importance attached to that issue by the party as well as the importance attached by the individual. It is the voter's "salience proximity" to a party in respect to a given issue that is supposed to lead to a vote for that party. Therefore information is required about the weight or priority that the issue is given on the political agenda of the party, and other parties.

Here, the most obvious sources of information are the party's platform

or program, or statements made by its leaders during the election campaign. But whether or not the voters have captured this information cannot be judged unless it is supplemented by survey evidence of how the voter
has perceived the stands of the parties. In the case of the trade-off items
this question is dealt with by letting the respondent judge the parties' positions, exactly as on policy issues. In the case of items on the importance of
various problems or goals, it is dealt with by letting the respondents judge
which political problems or goals were promoted by the individual parties.
For example, for each party one may ask the respondents what the party
talked about during the campaign.

The salience model specifically uses data on the election agenda to predict the aggregate election outcome. The logic of the salience model is that
one party is associated with one set of political goals or problems, another
party with another set, so that the respondent's goal preferences lead to a
choice between the parties. But if parties are associated with each a valence
issue, one might as well write the salience model in the simpler form,

Vote = a + b Salience of the party's issues,

which expresses that the more salient a particular issue becomes, the more
it will favour a particular party. Such a simple model is indeed presupposed
to work in many elections. For example, a green party automatically gets
more votes, the more environmental issues become salient in the election
campaign; or an anti-immigration party gets more votes, the more immigration becomes perceived as a threat to the national culture during the
months preceding the election. In the latter case, the model is used even
though the issue is in theory not a valence issue. For it is of course possible
to argue that the authorities should permit more immigrants to enter the
country. But advocates of this policy are so small a minority that we can assume that in practice the issue is a valence issue.

The consequences of such a model for party strategies differ very much
from party strategies on position issues. A difference between position
issues and valence issues is that a party may have position on all issues, but
it cannot declare all issues equally important. The party has limited resources during its campaign. It can decide to focus exclusively on one issue
or to spread its forces over several issues. But in terms of money for advert-
ising, TV time, and newspaper headlines, the party must decide among
issues. The size of the headlines and the space on the front pages of news-
papers are limited.

The same applies to the voter. Most voters' attention and memory are limited to a few aspects of the election. Thus if a new issue occupies the voter, it is more or less automatically traded off against other issues.

Under these conditions the best a party can hope for is that its "issue profile" closely matches the issue profile of a great many voters. Provided such data are at hand, one can measure the difference between the profiles of a given respondent and a given party and test a hypothesis that the more alike the two are, the more likely is it that the voter will support the party. Furthermore, issue by issue the difference between voters and a party can be treated as quasi-distances following the general issue voting model that was discussed in Chapter 2.

In theory such a saliency model should work on all valence issues, that is, whenever there is no question about which position to take on the issue. Of course it will not work on position issues; it does not make sense for someone who is interested in the abortion issue to vote for a party that emphasizes abortion unless one has the same stand as the party, either liberal or restrictive. But when the stand is implicit, as with unemployment or environmental protection, it may be surmised that a party attracts a particular issue public by emphasizing its concern over the problem.

An ambitious attempt to develop a saliency model that operates on the macro-level of election outcomes and rates of party support was launched by Budge and Farlie in *Explaining and Predicting Elections* in 1983. They claim that party competition is about making issues salient to the electorate rather than taking positions on these issues. Parties (or presidential candidates) do not actually debate controversial political goals or means; they talk past one another, each trying to set the political agenda for the election. A candidate who tries to confront the opponent's position on an issue will generally be disadvantaged because he implicitly admits the importance of the problem that the opponent mentions. Psychologically he shows willingness to play on the opponent's home ground. Superior tactics would be to change the game into one on which he is advantaged.

Budge and Farlie applied their model to postwar elections in 23 countries, distinguishing between a socialist/reforming and a conservative party or party group in each of these countries. According to their model, the party's share of the vote in an election would be a function of which types of issue were salient at the election. For this reason, fourteen types of issues were delimited and assigned weights from 1 (small effect) to 3 (large effect). The issue types were common to all elections and countries; some of them were believed to count positively for the socialist/reforming party, others to count positively for the conservative party, and still others to be erratic. For example, civil order or moral-religious issues counted +3 for the conservative party and –3 for the socialist/reforming party, whereas the reverse was the case with socioeconomic redistribution. Candidate reactions and government records counted in favour of whichever candidate or government was advantaged by the campaign communication, and according to the weight of that communication. Weights applied to elections in USA, Canada, and Ireland, differed somewhat but not decisively from those applied to the rest of the countries.

The observations, one for each party and election, was entered into the model,

Vote = a + b Issue score,

which states that the expected vote for the party was a (positive) function of its "issue score" in the election. The coefficient b varied of course from one country to the next but averaged around 0.9, indicating that the occurrence of an issue with a "large" effect increased the vote for the party by 2.7 percentage points. Naturally the coefficient a, which indicates the expected percentage voting for the party in the absence of issues, or in the case of a tie between positive and negative issues, also varied between parties.

In contrast to all the other models we have reviewed until now, the saliency model moves away from the individual level and to the aggregate level, treating the party's result at an election as one observation. In order to ensure a large set of observations it then becomes necessary to collect over-time or comparative data, preferably both. The model therefore fits well into the efforts to make election research more cumulative.

Nonetheless it must be seen as a weakness that these issue scores are not validated by survey data. Stemming from commentators of elections rather than from the voters themselves, a critical link in the electoral process is missing. Though commentators may have fingertip feelings for the effects of various issues on the vote, they are part of the political establishment and have been shown to be crucially wrong on several occasions. In this light, the authors' application of their model to predict ten elections held during the period 1977-79 (Budge and Farlie 1983, chap. 4) is fairly successful.

Conclusion

Issue priority, or issue salience, is a concept that permits the analysis of issue voting to be extended from position issues to valence issues. It appears to be particularly relevant when analyzing aggregated election outcomes because voters are more likely to be influenced by the media to rank an issue higher or lower in importance than to change their opinion on an issue. Thereby the election campaign often becomes a struggle for dominating the political agenda rather than converting people to the party's platform.

However, when the salience model is applied to individual voting behaviour, its power to predict the voting choice is usually not as great as that of most leading position issues. The salience model does not refer to policy alternatives that exclude one another. When respondents are asked how important a number of specified issues are, many of them will agree that practically all of these issues are important; they do not report which of them was foremost in their minds when they voted.

The salience model may well have its best prospect in the analysis of party images. Quite often, survey respondents are in strong agreement about what a party stands for – law and order, fighting pollution, cutting taxes, and so forth. When these images, and changes in them, are combined with macro-level accounts of the political agenda prior to an election, the result may well be a model of issue voting that competes successfully with the position model. This leads to the performance model that we shall now review.

Chapter 7

Retrospective Voting and Performance Voting

Retrospective Voting

So far we have focused on position issues, assuming that an election decides the policies and leadership of the coming period. The voters are assumed to consider the expected or future policy when they go to the polls. However it is obvious that many voters are not used to decision-making on such a scope. As we noted at the beginning of Chapter 2, issue voting, in the sense conceived by the Michigan researchers, was limited to the type of positional voting which poses fairly strict demands on the voter. The voter must select a position on every important issue, must be able to place the parties or presidential candidates reasonably correct, and must choose among the parties or candidates consistently in accordance with these positions. Most of the American electorate did not pass such a test; and for them the solution, according to the Michigan school, was to resort to candidate evaluations or party identification.

Among those objecting to this gloomy portrait of the American voter, the most important counter-argument was presented by V. O. Key, Jr., in *The Responsible Electorate* (1966). His argument was based on simple reward and punishment theory, that is, the hypothesis that an individual is likely to continue a behaviour which has rewarded him, and abandon a behaviour which has not proved rewarding. According to such a theory it would be possible for the electorate to pass judgment on the government simply by comparing the present with the past, noting whether life has improved or deteriorated during its period in power. Such result-oriented behaviour might even be more sensible than voting on the stands of the government and opposition because it would be based on facts rather than promises. Any candidate can promise a better future for the voter; the art is to fulfill such a promise, and the candidate or party should be judged according to its responsibility in that regard.

V. O. Key, Jr., illustrated his arguments with survey material from a string of presidential elections. Though his analysis controlled for former vote, a research design which we criticized in Chapter 2 for generating artificial issue effects, the group differences (effects) that he came up with were much too large to be written off as artificial. For a number of leading issues, the percent switching from one side to the other between elections was clearly associated with retrospective evaluations of the presidency. Governments that could boast about good results tended to conquer votes from the opposition in the net result, while governments that presented poor results tended to lose votes to the opposition.

For a decade and a half, retrospective voting was a side current in electoral research, until it was brought into the mainstream by Morris Fiorina in *Retrospective Voting in American National Elections* (1981). Using a sophisticated model of probit analysis, Fiorina regressed the presidential vote on respondents' positions on three or four leading retrospective issues for a number of American elections. For example, Nixon's 1960 vote was treated (pp. 36-37) as a function of five factors: (1) respondent's evalutions of whether there had been changes in the risk of a war, (2) changes in US relations with foreign countries, (3) changes in domestic affairs, (4) changes in the voter's personal financial situation, and (5) whether the respondent had been unemployed lately. All of these variables were shown to have significant effects on the presidential vote.

Clearly we are talking here about results rather than goals and policies. Distinguishing among voters with different goals becomes immaterial since everyone is supposed to have the same goal, namely, an improvement of national as well as personal conditions. Distinguishing between policy instruments for pursuing these goals is thought to be unimportant for the evaluation or vote: focussing on the result, the respondent is assumed not to care about how the result is achieved. The virtue is to base the choice on "realistic" rather than "idealistic" judgments.

But it should be noted that the distinction between retrospective voting and future-oriented (prospective) voting in principle cuts across the distinction between position issues and valence issues. Though the arguments of Key and Fiorina seem to limit the retrospective model to the analysis of valence issues, retrospective principles may apply to position issues as well. It is possible to ask, first, which position a respondent has taken on an issue, and second, to what extent the respondent thinks the government has pursued a policy that is close to that position. If the respondent denies this, it may be a plausible cause for voting for the opposition. If this means switching his vote, the respondent may defend himself by saying that the government promised to pursue the respondent's preferred policy but failed to do so.

Actually this is how Fiorina writes the retrospective model (pp. 66-68).

First, if none of the parties has been in government, simple issue voting takes place. The respondent compares the stands of the parties with respect to the benefits they offer, and chooses the one offering the largest improvement. However, once a party has governed, retrospective voting is added as a factor. The voter is now capable of balancing issue voting, which estimates future improvement, against retrospective voting, which estimates past improvements brought about by the government that is now running for re-election.

The decision process is easy to handle if we look at it from the perspective of the proximity model. We may then treat the retrospective evaluation simply as the proximity of the voter to the actual policy of the incumbent government. To illustrate, let us add the retrospective term to the proximity model and graph Fiorina's model as in Figure 7.1:

Figure 7.1. Positions of a Voter and Two Parties on an Issue Dimensions

Standing before election 2, the voter is located at position V_2, whereas the two parties are placed at positions P_2 and Q_2, respectively. If simple issue voting prevails, the voter will choose party P as the nearest party. However, P has been in government and during that time has conducted a policy, which is far from the voter and some way off from its present position; let us represent that policy by P_1. If retrospective voting prevails, the voter will disregard P_2 as being an empty promise – or, perhaps, a political goal which unfortunately cannot be fulfilled – and realize that Q_2 is nearer than the actual policy P_1 to his or her interest.

Downsian "proximity" analysis would not disregard the past, or current, policy of the government (P_1) as irrelevant for the vote. However, that policy is deemed relevant only because it is a better guide than P_2 to the government's future policy. V.O.Key's theory elevates past performance to a separate factor along the theory of learning: the electorate tends to repeat or continue behaviour that has brought rewards, and to discontinue and avoid behaviour that has brought harm.

Fiorina's model is more general and balances these possibilities by assuming that the voter may assign relative weights to P_1 and P_2. But there are several other ways to extend and modify the model. The voter may change position during the election campaign so as to move nearer to P_1, being persuaded that the actual policy is better than it seemed. The opposition party Q may not be trusted to fulfill its promises, so Q_2 is moved further to the left or the proximity to Q_2 devalued, leaving again the government party as the closer one; Fiorina speaks about a "reliability, uncertainty, or competency discount" (p. 73).

These modifications lead Fiorina toward a theory of party identification as a tally of past evaluation. The individual voter's identification with a governing party at election 2 can be conceptualized as the voter's party identification at election 1, modified by new evaluations due to the government's performance in the meantime. Again using the distance model for illustration, we may write:

Id with government party at election 2 = Id at election 1 + b Proximity to actual policy

where the last term refers to the distance between the voter's position in election 2 and government policy between election 1 and election 2. For example, a voter's Democratic party identification is hypothesized to be reinforced when distances between the voter and the Democratic party are kept low under Democratic presidencies. It is weakened if these distances are large, so that Democratic presidents disappoint their followers.

Over a long series of elections, party identification may be reconstructed as resulting from accumulated retrospective evaluations along the lines of the above equation. But for the analysis of a single election or short series of elections, changes in party identification seem relevant only when they are rapid and substantial. In that case they are interesting because they imply that a critical control variable, party identification, was itself affected by issue position of the "performance" type. Controlling for party identification in that case means over-controlling and thereby reducing the issue effect unnecessarily. Fiorina uses the panel of 1956-58-60 and 1972-74-76 to demonstrate that there is evidence of such feedback effects of certain issues on changes in party identification.

Hence we see that retrospective models can use positional issues as well as valence issues. This is most clearly the case with retrospective judgment of specific decisions made by a government on an issue. For example, the respondent is asked to evaluate whether Ford did right in giving Nixon pardon for his implication in the Watergate scandal, or whether the respondent supports the president's Vietnam policy. But most of the cases with which Fiorina illustrates his model are not positional. His leading example (1981, 71), actually has little to do with issue voting, since it deals with approval of Johnson's presidential job in 1968 and which party is perceived to be best in handling respondent's most important problem. The first is a non-issue and the second, not retrospective.

Retrospective judgments may be viewed as one way of getting information on the issues of prospective politics on which the voter reacts according to the position model. If a voter is uncertain about the "true" policy position of a party, and questions about its credibility are raised, the voter may try to remember which policy the party has actually pursued the last time it was in government. But does this mean that retrospective voting is more rational than prospective voting? To say that it is seems to be equivalent to saying that people should vote out of gratitude rather than base their vote on expectations. Actually there may be good reasons for trusting a party to change its policy if that policy has led to poor results in the past. Retrospective judgments should not be seen as a revolution in electoral theory but rather as a type of "empirical" evidence available to a voter who stands before the decision whether to vote for one government or another.

Performance Evaluations

The argument of Key, Fiorina, and others, that voters are result-oriented rather than goal-oriented, seems far more important than their argument that voters act retrospectively. This is because it attempts to extend the logic of issue voting to the government's performance on valence issues. For valence issues the voters are not supposed to advocate a certain policy. This they consider a job suitable for politicians, technicians, and administrators. The voters simply make judgments as to which team of leaders can best handle the various problems that the voters think are important. These capacities for handling problems and producing results in various policy areas are mentally rated and subsequently added up to a total point score for each team of leaders.

This is a rough description of the performance models. In terms of the consistency model we presented in Chapter 1, the performance model builds on the hypothesis that the higher the score a voter gives to the leaders of a party, the more likely he or she is to vote for that party. The analytic problem is to determine the impact of ratings in various issue areas on the sympathy for the party and the likelihood of voting for it. As part of their motivational or intellectual equipment, the leaders are judged as being competent in some areas and incompetent in others. The voters are therefore brought into a situation in which they must choose,

Table 7.1. Vote for Humphrey 1968, by foreign policy performance and party identification.

Party Identification	Party Preferred on Foreign Policy		
	Democrats	Same by Both	Republicans
Strong Democrats	92% (72)	85% (102)	50% (16)
Medium Democrats	87% (29)	56% (151)	29% (35)
Independents	72% (24)	28% (144)	4% (78)
Medium Republicans	50% (6)	9% (74)	7% (68)
Strong Republicans	... (0)	4% (27)	2% (85)

Source: Brody and Page (1972), p.451. No. of respondents in parentheses

for example, between a candidate who is competent in foreign policy and one who is competent domestic policies, or vice versa. An example is shown in Table 7.1.

The question on which the table was constructed was:

> Looking ahead, do you think the problem of keeping us out of a bigger war would be handled better in the next four years by the Democrats, by the Republicans, or about the same by both?

Obviously, to answer such a question the respondent need not know anything about the foreign policy positions of the two parties. We can safely assume, however, that every American, including the leaders of the two parties, wants to keep his country out of a bigger war. Thus the item is a valence issue. Still, we may define the position of those in the left-hand column to be closer to the Democratic position than to the Republican position, whereas the reverse is true of those in the right-hand column. Those in the middle column are defined as located midway between the Democratic and Republican positions. The logic of the proximity model still applies in this case, as we expect the respondents to weigh their proximity to the two parties on various issues and choose the nearest.

However, a difference from positional issues is that the question invites the respondents to rationalize their party choice. As was the case with the positional items of type 3 in our typology in chapter 2, the performance issues shortcut the thought process associated with issue voting. The issue positions are said to be *mediated* by the parties. In the case of mediated variables it is especially important to demonstrate that they have an effect on the vote beyond the effect of party loyalty, hence the control for party identification in the table.

The vote for Hubert Humphrey varies from 92 percent in the upper left cell to 2 percent in the lower right. It is obvious that this variation is caused by differences in both party identification and performance evaluation. Indeed, the variation that is due to performance evaluation appears at first glance to be of the same order of magnitude as the part due to party identification, since the column differences range between 40 and 70 percent. However, the Ns in parentheses reveal that party identification and performance evaluations are rather closely correlated. As a background variable, party identification therefore has a considerable direct influence as well as a considerable indirect influence (via performance evaluation) on the vote.

Danish data. All the same, such a research finding is stimulating to those who believe that performance evaluations are important factors in voting behaviour, perhaps just as important for electoral change as are changes in public opinion. It is therefore worthwhile to see whether they generalize to other countries. As for the Danish data, Table 7.2 indicates that the situation is much the same as in the US electorate.

Table 7.2. Vote for the Danish government 1994. By party identification and ratings on the issue of tax burden vs social welfare

| Party Identification | Ability to solve Generel Economic Problems | | | |
	Present government best	No dif- ference	Bourgeois goverment best	All
Identifies with a government party	99% (197)	96% (135)	94% (65)	97% (397)
Feels closer to a government party	99% (74)	90% (109)	79% (81)	89% (264)
Does not feel close to any party	61% (33)	51% (75)	30% (113)	42% (221)
Feels closer to a non-government party	20% (40)	19% (70)	6% (231)	10% (341)
Identifies with a non-government party	4% (50)	0% (64)	1% (415)	2% (529)
All	76% (397)	62% (457)	20% (916)	43% (1770)

In this case, the respondent was asked who he/she thought was best at solving the country's general economic problems: either the present government, which was dominated by the Social Democrats, or a bourgeois government. It is observed that the difference between the two opposite groups of party identifiers, the first and the fifth row, is very large, very few identifiers of one party bloc voting for the opposite bloc. However there is space for considerable differences in the middle rows between those who evaluate the government more positively and those who evaluate an alternative government more positively.

In such a case logistic regression is obviously preferable to linear regression if we want to compress all of the information in one function. Let us code the five levels of party identification from +1=identifies with a government party, to -1=identifies with an opposition; and let us code performance evaluation from +1=present government best, to –1=bourgeois government best. The logistic regression function will then be

Log odds of government vote = 3.89 Party identification + 1.06 Performance evaluation – 0.47.

We find that the effect of party identification is three to four times that of performance evaluation. However, the latter is also significant. If the regression curve is estimated for performance evaluation alone, leaving out party identification, the effect is 1.44, whereas the effect of party identification alone is 4.05. Party identification control is obviously necessary in order to obtain a realistic impression of how performance evaluations influence the vote, but it is difficult to maintain, in the face of this evidence, that performance evaluations reflect nothing but party preference or party loyalty.

Performance and Electoral Change

Party strategies under the performance model may be expected to focus on the "images" of the parties, especially when they are in government. A party which acquires a good image, say, for economic restraint, may be expected to do particularly well when a great deal of the electorate feel the need for economic restraint – but less well when the economy is working well and the electors feel the need for improving social services. Just as, in the positional model, it is possible for a party to attract voters to its ideological positions, it is possible, in the policy evaluation model, for a party or leadership team to 'specialize' in solving particular problems, such as inflation, threats of war, or social inequality. A division of labour between two parties or government coalitions may then emerge such that the nature of the national problems determines which government is preferred by the public. Different problems call for different leaders.

To what extent does the government's performance on economic and other issues determine the election outcome? It seems likely that performance factors on valence issues are even more important than position changes in affecting the destiny of governments. Contrary to what was assumed in the salience model that we discussed in the foregoing chapter, it is possible for a party to change its image by displaying success in handling a foreign-policy situation or social and economic problems. To continue our example in Table 7.2, we show in Table 7.3 the vote for the Danish Social Democratic Party in 1994 and 1998 according to the voters' evaluations of how capable the two competing governments are in solving the country's general economic problems.

Table 7.3. Vote for the Danish Social Democratic Party 1994 and 1998. By performance evaluations on general economic problems

	1994	1998	Change
Vote for SD Party			
Present government best	71%	70%	-1%
No difference, or don't know	49	38	-11
Bourgeois government best	10	7	-3
All	34%	35%	+1%
Distribution of opinion			
Present government best	22%	35%	+13%
No difference, or don't know	26	28	+2
Bourgeois government best	52	37	-15
Total	100%	100%	

Note. Responses to the question, "We want to hear who you think is best at solving the problems I shall now read to you, either the present government led by Social Democrats, or a bourgeois government. Who is best at solving the country's general economic problems?"

We find in the upper part of the table that the Social Democrats lost support in all three categories of voters and particularly in the neutral catgory. Yet the party increased its aggregated support slightly from 34 to 35 percent. The explanation is found in the lower section of the table, which shows that the party's image compared with that of the bourgeois parties had improved considerably from 1994 to 1998. In 1994 more than twice as many believed the bourgeois government to be superior than those who believed the Social Democratic government to be superior; in 1998 the two sides were balanced in public perceptions. One can compute from these figures that if the opinion distribution had not changed from 1994 to 1998, the Social Democratic Party would have decreased from 34 to 29 percent of the vote instead of going up to 35 percent. The change in the party's image, relative to that of the competing government, as manager of the economy meant a difference of six percent of the vote cast.

Combining Salience and Performance: Issue Ownership

In an important sense, the salience model and the performance model complement one another. According to the salience model, the performance of each party in a future situation is more or less given, and what differs from one election to the next is the relevance of the problem or issue on which the parties are supposed to perform. According to the performance model, the economy and a few other issues are the permanent concerns of all voters, and what differs from one election to the next is that parties can improve or weaken their images as competent leaders in handling these eternal problems. It seems therefore that the two models may profit from combining their forces, thereby devising a more complete model. The fact or feeling that a certain problem is immanent is no help to the voter before he or she can connect the solution of that problem with a particular party, which means chiefly connecting it with the party's performance. Conversely, the fact that a certain party has a good record in solving certain problems will naturally be more relevant for the voter's choice, the more pressing the problem is.

When parties are firmly identified with particular issues we may speak of issue ownership (Petrocik 1996). Propagating the issue in that case means acquiring votes for the party. Party strategy becomes a game in which the party decides which of its own issues to emphasize in the present campaign. Concentrating on one issue runs the risk that the issue "dies" in the course of the campaign because the electors find it irrelevant. Spreading its forces over several issues entails that the voters get confused and do not capture the message. And, of course, campaigning on issues that belong to the opposite party risks playing into the hands of the opposition.

The theory of issue ownership seems to disregard the possibility that parties are chosen because of their positions on divisive issues. The respondents are not supposed, or asked, to change opinion under the campaign, only to re-assess the saliency of the prevailing issues. In principle a socialist voter may be induced to vote for a conservative party because he or she does not think the election is about socialism or conservatism but about a theme on which the conservative party happens to be nearer to his own position. On the other hand, occasionally socialist governments conduct conservative policies or vice versa when the situation demands it, or when it appears feasible. A party may borrow another party's issue, arguing, for example, that the other party has failed to solve a problem within its supposed field of competence.

A test of the issue ownership model on nine US presidential elections was conducted by John Petrocik (1996). He classified the problems (issues) into pro-Democratic and pro-Republican ones according to which party was generally perceived to be better in handling that problem. For example, on protecting social security or solving farm problems the Democrats were considered by most voters to be better, so that issue was classified as pro-Democratic. On holding down taxes or combating crime, the majority considered the Republicans to be better in handling the problem, so these problems were classified as pro-Republican. Next, for each election he computed the percent of the sample that were concerned mostly with pro-Democratic issues minus the percent that were concerned mostly with pro-Republican issues. He obtained a fair, though not impressive, positive correlation between the issue score so computed and the Democratic vote.

It is perhaps not fair to stress the mediocrity of this finding because the deviations from the best-fitting line are more interesting than the vote it predicts. Some campaigns focus on the government's performance on both its owns and the opposition's issues; the opposition may borrow an issue which is owned by the government if that issue has been handled poorly. Petrocik shows that this was the case in the Carter-Reagan duel in 1980. Here, Carter was disadvantaged by his putatively poor handling of not only Republican-owned issues (inflation and Iran) but also Democratic-owned issues (unemployment). The result is that his vote fell far below the one predicted from the balance of pro-Democratic and pro-Republican issues in the campaign.

As another case, Krosnick and Kinder (1990) showed that approval of Reagan declined from 65 to 45 percent after the Iran/Contra scandal in late 1986, and that the decline was related to the more general attitude of isolationism. Thus, on an issue thought to profit the Republican side, the Democrats could profit. In a situation where an issue becomes highly salient, the parties' images in respect to performance may change rapidly.

The issue ownership theory of Petrocik assumes that the parties' handling images may change, even within an election campaign (when one party borrows the issue from the other). The salient issues are determined by "priming" and "framing" the issues, for example by media headline news which are employed by the candidates to position themselves vis-a-vis the voters early in the campaign. These may well generate changes in the performance variable, such as we saw in Table 7.3. During the 1980 election campaign, the Reagan forces skillfully exploited the bad news about Carter's administration, so that "The Republican tone of the election was so overwhelming that the Democrats did not even dominate their issues." (Petrocik 1996, 841). The two most prominent issues were the economy (right after the 1979 oil crisis) and foreign policy (the hostages in Teheran), both of which counted in favour of the Republicans.

The issue ownership model is a model of the election campaign. Its focus is on the tactical use of events and opportunities, on the treatment of issues in news stories rather than the issues themselves. We have come a long way from the serene structure of ideological issues with which we began in Table 2.1. Furthermore, the issue ownership model, like the saliency model, is a model of the election outcome; it treats the aggregated electorate as observations. In contrast to the salience model it utilizes voter perceptions and attitudes, rather than texts containing party platforms or judgments made by commentators, to model the vote. Still, even the issue ownership model makes little use of survey material. It assumes, for example, that issue salience and perceived handling capabilities are the same for all respondents of a survey, and that they result in a certain probability of voting for a given party. This probability applies to all respondents. It would be an improvement to drop this assumption. Those voters who find an issue very important may well have a different impression of the party's or government's performance than those who find the issue unimportant. Thus the notion of different "issue publics" should be incorporated to make the issue ownership model more sophisticated.

Economic Voting

In the performance model, the main issue is whether the government has done a good job or a bad job in respect to a specified policy area. It is only a small step to omit any reference to the government in asking whether the state of affairs in that area is satisfactory or not, or whether it is improving or deteriorating. This way of making the question unmediated may contribute to remove part of the perceptual screen that causes the strong correlation with party identification (cf. Table 7.1 or 7.2). If so desired, the researcher may follow up with a question as to whether the putative good or bad state of affairs is the government's desert or fault, respectively, and whether a different government would have made any difference.

By far the most widely used questions of this sort deal with economic indicators such as inflation, unemployment, economic growth or the foreign trade balance. They are analyzed in the large number of sophisticated studies using econometric methods. These studies are competently reviewed elsewhere (see. eg, Lewin 1991; Nannestad and Paldam 1994; Lewis-Beck 1988; Hibbs 1993), and only a brief summary will be given here.

In the early 1970s the field of economic voting, or economic effects on government support as indicated by opinion polls, was pioneered by Goodhart & Bhansali (1970) in the case of British government popularity and by Kramer (1971) in the case of US congressional elections. Their articles triggered a great number of studies yielding a mixed bag of information on the effect of the economic variables.

The studies in this tradition do not use information about individual voters and therefore is not concerned with the problem of how people reacted to the issues, but the estimated effects were at least implicitly assumed to stem from people voting their "pocketbooks". This assumption was seriously challenged when Kinder and Kiewiet (1979) published a study to show that voting was "sociotropic", that is, people reacting to their perception of the national economy rather than to their own economy. For cross-sectional studies, this hypothesis has generally held up (cf. Lewis-Beck 1990; Lewin 1991). In Lewis-Beck's comparative study of five European countries, based on the Eurobarometer survey, the simple retrospective items on the personal and collective income development ran:

How does the financial situation of your household at present compare to what it was 12 months ago?

> How do you think the general economic situation in this country has changed over the last 12 months?

Both items called for five-way responses (a lot better, better, same, a little worse, a lot worse). Thus it is possible to make a strict comparison between their effects on the vote intention. And in this comparison the collective, or "sociotropic", item fared best. For five countries – Britain, France, West Germany, Italy and Spain – the mean correlation with the intended vote for the government party or parties was r=0.18 for the personal item and r=0.36 for the collective item (Lewis-Beck 1990, 49). And when both items were entered into a regression model, the personal item disappeared into insignificance in each of the five countries (*ibid.* p.56). Its effect was eclipsed by the collective item, just as in the Kinder and Kiewiet (1979) study of the United States.

In Lewis-Beck's design, ideological self-placement on a left-right scale provides a control for the respondent's general political predisposition. Thus the effects he measures are vote intention differences associated with differences in people's evaluations of the collective economy, for voters on the ideological left, center, and right. This is a very strong control, and consequently it is difficult to deny that he demonstrates the impact of the good or bad state of the national economy on the voting choice.

Sociotropic effects in this sense are not causal in the sense that the vote for government is influenced by the state of the national economy, only by respondents' perceptions of that state. Respondents are of course influenced in these perceptions by news headlines and other communications as well as by their partisan predisposition. The effects are issue effects similar to those we have discussed until now. By contrast, personal, or "egotropic", variables are not issues but analogous to social background variables.

Sociotropic versus Policy Voting

The sociotropic hypothesis in economic voting may be generalized to a hypothesis stating that voters reward or punish their governments according to how they perceive the state and development of society in various issue areas. How does this model of issue voting compare with the policy model we have reviewed in previous chapters?

In various surveys we find voter perceptions of the national situation or trend to be gauged by questions such as, "Do you think the chance of getting into a war has increased or decreased during the past year?" or, "Do you think that the natural environment in this country has improved or deteriorated in the last years?" or even, "Do you think moral standards are deteriorating?" A positive view of the situation or development is then hypothesized to have a positive effect on the vote for the government which has presided over the period surveyed, especially of course if the issue has ignited public debate during the election campaign.

The British surveys are especially rich in these questions. Let us see how the sociotropic model works in the case of the British 1997 election, which had all the appearance of a people passing a negative judgment on its government. Concerning the development since last election, the respondents were asked seven questions of the type, "Would you say that since then unemployment has increased or fallen?" Opinions were predominantly negative. 86 percent thought prices had risen and only 4 percent, that they had fallen. 81 percent thought crime had risen, while only 9 percent thought it had fallen. 77 percent thought health standards had fallen, while 11 percent thought they had risen. 65 percent thought that educational standards had fallen, while 15 percent thought they had risen. Only on the issues of unemployment and general standards of living, opinions were more divided: 46 percent thought that unemployment had increased, as against 43 percent who thought it had fallen; and 30 percent thought that living standards had risen, while another 30 percent thought they had fallen. On this last question, a full 40 percent thought that no change had taken place.

The wording of these questions should be carefully noted. Prior to the item series, the respondent was reminded that the 1992 election was "the one where John Major won against Neil Kinnock". This may well have cued the respondents to take a more positive view of the development if they were Conservative identifiers, a more negative view if they were Labour identifiers. However, as we have just seen, it is characteristic that public evaluations differ from one issue area to the next. Therefore the questions cannot be highly leading – at least not as leading as the performance items we reviewed earlier in the chapter.

In order to test the sociotropic model, we may estimate a regression model of the form

$$\text{Conservative vote} = a + b_1 \, \text{Development 1} + \ldots + b_7 \, \text{Development 7,}$$

in which Development 1 to Development 7 stand for the development in the seven areas, measured on a scale from +2 (most positive) to -2 (most negative). The result is a fair relationship with a multiple correlation coefficient of 0.57. The strongest negative effects on the Conservative vote are noted for the rise in unemployment, the decline of health standards and living standards, and the rise in taxes.

Thus the success of the sociotropic model in Britain is as great as that of the most successful position models we have studied so far. The two types of model can be freely mixed, of course, since it is perfectly logical to argue that a voter will vote for the Conservative government either (a) if he or she agrees with the policy aims of the party, or (b) if he or she recognizes that things have gone the right way during the government's tenure. If the voter disagrees on one of these points, there is a real dilemma as to whether one should vote out of "ideological" or "pragmatic" reasons.

Using three indicators from each of these models, the standardized issue effects in a regression analysis of the English survey respondents was:

Conservative vote = 0.30 Development of unemployment
              + 0.12 Development of taxes
              + 0.06 Development of prices
              + 0.19 Attitude to redistribution
              + 0.10 Attitude to taxes/spending
              + 0.07 Attitude to nationalization/privatization,

with a multiple correlation coefficient of 0.54. Hence it appears that the most efficient predictors of the government vote was the perception of how the rate of unemployment was going, and the attitude to income redistribution. Somewhat less important were the perception of whether taxes had gone up or down, and the opinion on whether they *ought* to go up or down. Even less important was the perception of price development, and the opinion on nationalization or privatization.

The conclusion is that the two types of model are fairly balanced in respect to strength. This suggests that items on social trends ought to be more prominent than they are at present in national election surveys, insofar as these surveys aim to explain the fortune of governments.

Conclusion

Performance variables, being often "mediated" variables, are likely to be heavily influenced by party identification and ideological bias. Still, they generally do have independent effects on the vote. Parties, as well as their leaders, do have "images" of competence or success in dealing with different issue areas, and voters react to these images. This is seen most clearly when the same survey questions have been asked at successive elections. The increase or decrease in support for a party may then be decomposed into changes in the competence image and changes in the effect of these images on the vote.

The study of how the economic and social development is perceived, and how this affects the vote, is an extremely interesting extension of issue voting, especially as it provides a link between political science on the one hand, and economics and sociology on the other. At present this field of study suffers from a lack of overtime data which extends over a considerable period, except in respect to economic development. The glimpses of the data we have seen suggest that "sociotropic" variables tend to override "egotropic" ones and compete successfully with changes in party positions and changes in public opinion in explaining the vote for governments and leading opposition parties.

Chapter 8

The Causes of Issue Voting

The foregoing chapters have mostly discussed the mechanism of issue voting. The perspective in the last chapter shifts to the broader context of issue voting. The aim is to empirically study the circumstances under which the parameters of issue voting models change under the impact of forces external to these models, and to evaluate the hypotheses in this field.

The consistency model we introduced in Chapter 1 described the interplay between the voter's issue orientation (V), a party's issue orientation (P), and the voter's attitude (A) to the party. The main objective of the model was to determine A as a function of V and P. But we did not discuss how external forces could intrude in this model to change either V or P. How do voters acquire issue orientations independently of their partisan attitudes? How do they acquire information about the issue positions of the parties and about the policy of the government? What causes parties to change their stands on issues? These questions take us to broader topics of opinion formation and cognition on the one hand, and party strategies on the other. To be complete, a theory of issue voting should attempt to answer questions of the following kind: Under what circumstances will a certain issue emerge? How will the public be divided on the issue? How will the government and various other parties react to it? And what will be the outcome of the debate in the short as well as the long term? In this chapter we briefly discuss some of the hypotheses pertaining to these questions.

Self-Interest or Symbolic Politics?

How do voters acquire their issue positions? Before survey researchers began to ask questions about the voters' issue orientations, this did not seem to be a major problem. Socioeconomic models of the electorate were built on information about the voter's occupation, income, age, trade union membership, racial and religious characteristics, in addition to the voting choice. In these models the gap between social position and political choice was bridged by means of assumptions about self-interest and about whose interests were served by different parties. For example it was thought to be rational for a working-class voter to vote for a socialist party that worked for higher wages; maybe it was also rational for an ardent church-goer to vote for a religious party.

It is true that these models, based on relatively fixed characteristics, did not account for short-run change in election outcomes. But it was possible to remedy this lack by supplementing them with *ad hoc* explanations. For example, one might show that the socialist party had lost voters in a concrete election especially among those workers who were church-goers. However, during the 1960s these social cleavages began to be undermined, the correlation between party choice on the one hand, and class and religion on the other, dropping consistently over time. The notion of "catch-all" parties was invoked to explain this phenomenon; without the aid of attitude measurement it was impossible to come up with more constructive notions for the change that took place. The ideological party was declared dead, and in its place, the pragmatic party, which cared for all groups almost equally, was born. To account for electoral change, the government's vote was shown to depend on its success in generating high employment, price stability, and economic growth.

The development and spread of survey techniques have changed our views on voter rationality in this simple sense. Concerning occupational voting, for example, we have witnessed in the British case that already in 1964, the vote was strongly dependent on ideological attitudes, even after social class controls. In the field of economic voting, as we noted in Chapter 7, the hypothesis of "pocket-book" voting normally is inferior to the hypothesis of "sociotropic voting", in which the voter evaluates the national economic development along the lines prescribed by a model of issue voting. In this light, the Kinder and Kiewiet article in 1979 can be seen as a reaction against a too rationalistic view of voting.

In the same year David Sears and his associates launched a more direct attack on the theory of self-interest in voting behaviour. Drawing upon Murray Edelman's *Politics as Symbolic Action* (1971), they produced data to show that people react negatively on issues which contain negative symbols even if such a reaction runs against their economic interests. For example, those white parents who were opposed to school busing were shown not particularly to live in districts where there were plans to introduce school busing; rather, these parents had grown up in families with racial prejudice (Sears, Hensler, and Speer 1979). The researchers also pointed out that symbolic issues had had a major impact on the presidential vote of 1972 (Sears, Lau, Tyler and Allen 1980).

In the model of issue voting we have explored, self-interest applies at different points. We may apply it to the *saliency* variable, arguing that, for example, the issue of old age pensions should be more important for older voters than for the young. We may apply it to *issue positions*, arguing that older voters should be more favourable than younger ones to an increase in old age pensions. And we may apply it to *party preferences*, arguing that those who want old age pensions to be increased should be more favourable than other voters to parties that campaign for an increase in old age pensions. The proximity theory, with which we began Chapter 2, for all its emphasis on rationality, does not prescribe what issue positions the voter should choose, or what importance to attach to these issues, merely that once taken, these positions should lead to a vote for the nearest party. A voter may choose a self-defeating position and still behave in accordance with the proximity theory. In fact, by the standards of proximity theory, Sears' racially prejudiced voter is more rational than one who decides *not* to let his prejudice dominate his voting choice.

It would be interesting to study the behaviour of voters whose objective self-interest dictates one position on an issue, but whose actual position is a different one. From our models we should anticipate that the actual position almost always will be the more important in terms of its effect on the vote. The notion of self-interested issue positions appears fruitful as it may raise new and interesting problems for research, such as: who are the irrational voters? And how do they react when their preferred policy is carried out to the disadvantage of themselves?

Affect and Cognition

Rationality, whether of the self-interest variety or not, also requires that voters choose issue positions after having considered their implications: cognition logically precedes evaluation and affect. On this point, the line attacking rationality in issue voting was continued from a slightly different psychological angle in the second half of the 1980s. In 1980 the social psychologist Robert Zajonc had claimed that "preferences need no inferences". He found that "affect and cognition constitute distinguishable, independent systems of evaluation" (Zajonc 1980), and that "affective judgments tend to be more enduring and less vulnerable to persuasion than cognitive judgments" (*ibid.*). Subsequently Pamela Conover and Stanley Feldman (1986) showed that affective reactions to issues played an independent role in influencing the partisan choice. As they recapitulate (Conover and Feldman 1986, 50):

Our results indicate that (1) positive and negative reactions to the economy are
to a certain degree independent; (2) affective and cognitive reactions to
economic conditions are only weakly correlated, especially on the national
level; and (3) emotional reactions to both personal and national economic
conditions are important in explaining political evaluations"

Specifically, their factor analysis revealed three factors, one for positive and
two for negative emotions. The positive factor represented feelings of being
hopeful, proud, confident, and happy. The first negative factor represented
feeling angry, disgusted and frustrated; the second, feeling afraid, uneasy,
and (again) frustrated.

Their findings may explain why the pocket-book effect differs from one
group of voters to the next and sometimes seems to vanish altogether.
Some voters may not blame their government for their loss of income; for
example, Brody and Sniderman (1977) found a tendency among American
voters to overcome economic crises by means of an "ethos of self-reliability". As for those who do blame their government, media-generated and
group-generated feelings of injustice probably vary a lot. If indeed affect
and cognition are only weakly associated with one another, proximity theory might suggest a sort of "double-barrelled" approach, by which a voter's
anger, fear, or other types of affect leads to one issue position, whereas
pragmatic interest based on information leads to another. Moreover, even
when the position actually taken seems dictated by self-interest and knowledge, it may not favour the "nearest" party because that party arouses
negative affect for other reasons.

The recognition that affect is a force which may supersede rational calculation seems consistent with the directional theory of issue voting, which
we reviewed in Chapter 4, than with proximity theory. This is because directional theory postulates that what matters is not whether the voter position is similar to the party position, but whether affect is aroused when
the subject of the attitude is confronted with the object of the attitude.

The problem with the concept of symbolic voting is that it is difficult to
measure and that it seems to cover several non-rational types of behaviour. A
general division of motives into four types seems warranted by the *functional*
theory of attitudes (Katz 1960). According to that theory, attitudes may
serve four main functions: the knowledge, pragmatic, symbolic, and ego-
defensive functions. In consequence of such a distinction, pragmatic self-
interest may be superseded by an ideological need for understanding, cognitive consistency, and knowledge; or by the need for symbolically expressing
traditional – religious, national or ethnic – belonging to a certain group.

This entails that one should distinguish as sharply as possible between symbolic and ideological voting, two main types that are not self-interested behaviour but very different on other points. Symbolic voting may be used to explain sudden panics or waves of enthusiasm. Ideological voting can explain quite the opposite phenomenon, namely, the rigidity in voter positions and party images that we have noticed throughout the previous chapters. They lead to widely different perspectives on issue voting in the future.

The Theory of Cognitive Mobilization

It is often held that present-day voters differ characteristically from voters of the past in being more sensitive to policy differences and better informed about them on the average. Franklin (1985) argues this point in the case of the British electorate; Inglehart (1990) talks about a development from elite-directing to elite-directed politics; and Dalton, Flanagan and Beck (1984) speak about a theory of cognitive mobilization of the electorates of modern societies. According to Dalton (1988, 21).

> Cognitive mobilization involves two separate developments. First, there has been a decrease in the cost of acquiring information about politics. Second, there has been an increase in the public's ability to process political information. Cognitive mobilization thus means that more citizens now have the political resources and skills necessary to deal with the complexities of politics and make their own political decisions.

The level of cognitive mobilization may be measured by political knowledge, by political interest, or by participation in the campaign either as discussant or as exposure to mass media communication about politics. More external to politics, it may be measured as length of school education. In any case the idea is that the information-handling capacity of the voter generates a tendency toward issue voting, and that this capacity shows a rising trend in modern societies.

In most cases it is true that informed citizens display a higher correlation than uninformed citizens between issue position and party preference. An example is the VP correlation we found in Chapter 2, Table 2.7. There, the Conservative vote was found to vary more with issue position among the well-educated than among those with shorter education. Similarly we found by regression methods that political interest interacted with issue position to create a stronger issue effect among those with a great deal of interest than among those with little or no interest in politics.

However, issues differ very much in respect to how much information it requires to take a consistent stand and related this stand to the parties. Carmines and Stimson (1980) point out that there are "two faces of issue voting". Technical, or what they call "hard" issues do require information, but not "easy" issues such as racial segregation. For the 1972 election they find that on the Vietnam issue, squared etas for predicting issue position from party preference varied from 0.15 among uninformed to 0.46 among highly informed voters. On racial segregation, it varied unsystematically from 0.06 among the least informed to 0.17 in the middle group and only 0.11 among the most informed group.

It is clear that "easy" issues are similar to what Edelman and Sears call symbolic issues. "Hard" issues are either pragmatic or ideological, but not necessarily issues with a high content of self-interest. The distinction therefore seems to be the type of schema that is applied to the voting decision: whether it is a simple ingroup/outgroup schema or a more advanced one. As we discussed in Chapter 7, politically informed and well-educated voters tend to use the left-right schema or other types of spatial schemas to differentiate between political objects. Thus, the two faces of issue voting are an admonition that a high level of issue voting may not be a blessing for the democratic process. That will depend on the type of issues that dominate the election.

The theory of cognitive mobilization therefore paints a too optimistic picture of future of citizen politics. It is true that the higher general level of education that has characterized development since the 1950s can be expected to lead to a higher amount of issue voting. Such a rise in issue voting is also consistent with the greater importance of the public sector and of improved communication facilities in modern societies, as well as a declining need for parties as organizations for political socialization and recruitment of leaders. All of these features of modern society combine into the notion that postindustrial societies are characterized by a large proportion of active and critical voters who turn to issue voting as the main mechanism for controlling political decisions. But the darker side is that postindustrial society also offers an opportunity for symbolic politics and waves of panic.

New Politics Theory and Issue Voting

Postindustrial theory stresses the increasing role of information and service occupation, as well as the change in work organization, from the routine work in factory organization toward creative work in professional organizations, that is taking place in modern societies. This change is supposed to promote New Politics issues at the cost of traditional left-right issues, or what Inglehart describes as a reduced "marginal utility of economic values" (Inglehart 1990, chap. 6). More precisely, the Norwegian scholar A. Todal Jenssen (1993) has described it as a choice between two types of "relational values". The factory organization promoted hierarchical power values and short-run self-interested behaviour. The professional organization promotes cooperation and egalitarian values.

Postindustrial theory leads to the hypothesis that issue voting on Old Politics issues will decline while issue voting on New Politics issues will increase. As regards the former, we have just reviewed the evidence. As for the rise of New Politics issues, this seems substantiated in a number of countries, particularly those in which green parties emerged in the 1970s and anti-immigration parties in the 1980s. In the case of Germany, one researcher concluded in connection with the 1987 election that the themes of environmental protection and nuclear power increased in importance (without, however, a corresponding loss in importance for the old economic themes) (Kuechler 1990, 431). Furthermore, there is evidence that party identifications continued to decline (Dalton and Rohrschneider 1990).

The later development has been completely dominated by the reunion of West and East Germany. This has given rise to a theory of two sets of issue orientations operating side by side in the same election (Rohrschneider and Fuchs 1998; Fuchs and Rohrschneider 1998), one materialist in East Germany and a rather more postmaterialist in West Germany.

But it is ironic that postmaterial theory largely has been right in predicting a rise in New Politics issue voting, at the same time that it has been wrong in identifying the relevant issues. It has pointed to issues of minority rights and quality of life, but it has failed to take into account the reaction coming from the industrial and preindustrial formations in society. The New Right, which grew up during the 1980s in reaction against the New Left, also vote on non-material issues, though on issues such as immigration, crime, and abortion. These issues represent the problems, rather than the perspectives, associated with the coming of postindustrial society.

In this connection it is worth noting that in New Politics theory, the educated sectors of society play a double role, both as promoters of new values and as promoters of issue voting generally. In terms of our consistency model of issue voting (cf. Chapter 1), education should affect both V and the VP correlation, that is, well-educated voters not only have specific issue orientations but also the resources to translate these into a consistent party choice. Hence it follows that their issue positions are likely to become over-represented in government policies. In that case, however, New Politics theory may entail a new type of class conflict between higher and lower levels of education, rather than a general rise in issue voting.

The prediction that Old Politics issues were obsolete in postindustrial society has not been too successful either. The new liberalism of the 1980s, which countered an ideology of public spending and welfare services by an ideology of free markets and global competition, raised the level of issue voting in many countries. On that backdrop it would not be unnatural to expect the effect of economic issues to decline somewhat, when a partial consensus had emerged in the following decade. But the tendency of non-economic issues to take over and produce violent issue effects has been less consistent than one might expect from the theories of value change, new politics, and participant voters. Some of these issues have been promoted by parties that are as yet playing a marginal role in the parliaments and in government policy: on the one side, the green parties, and on the other side, the anti-immigration parties. Their support has served as "barometers" of social problems to which the major parties therefore have had to respond. But no cataclysmic new cleavages have developed to overturn the traditional party systems (except in Italy, and for other reasons). In most other systems, the new issues have typically caused instability and deviating elections. The alternation of bourgeois and labour governments has continud into the 1990s, with the latter gradually prevailing in most of Western Europe.

A Rise in Issue Voting?

As noted already in our introduction, the early election studies up until the first half of the 1970s showed little concern for issue voting, whereas the later studies have increasingly focused on issue voting. This has led to a tendency to see issue voting as perpetually rising in modern societies. The participant voter scenario is a child of the late 1960s and early 1970s, when issue voting was "rediscovered" primarily by American researchers; but it was eagerly seized by their European colleagues, as it fit well with the picture of declining class and party loyalties observed among the voters. The space left by long-term forces was supposed to be occupied by short-term forces making way for new parties and social movements, which in turn caused a greater volatility in the party systems.

Issue voting is predicted by these theories to display a long-range increase. What is the evidence of the 1980s and 1990s for such a trend? For

Britain, Franklin (1985b) estimated the effect of issues, as a proportion of all impacts on the individual vote, to have risen from 25 percent in 1964 to the level of 40 percent in 1979 and 1983. He thought it "reasonable to hypothesize that the decline of class voting will have opened the way, at least to a limited extent, for a rise in issue voting to take place" (p. 38). In 1983, the issue of nuclear defence was added to the perennial issues of nationalization and welfare as factors affecting the vote; and on the economic issues, the Labour Party and the Conservative party polarized their positions visibly. This also seems to have been felt by the voters. In the 1983 and 1987 surveys, 84-85 percent of the respondents perceived a "very great" difference between the parties in regard to issue positions. This was a jump from 48 percent in 1979, and by 1992 the level was back to 56 percent (Heath et al. 1991; Norris 1997, 159). Norris concludes (161) "that the traditional left-right Labour and Conservative battle over the economy and the welfare state clearly outweighs major party competition over international affairs."

This seems also to be the case in the 1990s. In the 1992 election survey, in constructing an issue voting model, we find the strongest issues to be the classical economic issues of nationalization, redistribution, and welfare services. At a lower level, issues touching on the new politics dimension (nuclear power, the death penalty, and the rights of homosexuals) exert a significant impact on the Conservative vote, less on the Labour vote. By adding issues to the regression model it is possible to bring the multiple correlation up to 0.61 in the case of the Conservative vote and 0.54 in the case of the Labour vote.

However, we do not find that the British data point to a rise of issue voting on traditional economic issues since the 1960s. The British election file contains some issue data that reaches back to the 1960s, including the nationalization versus privatization issue. Extending the issue voting model with social class controls and applying it to a succession of elections, we find a level of issue voting which has not changed systematically over the years. The uncontrolled effect, or correlation, is similar in the 1990s to what it was in the 1960s. The same can be said for the class-controlled effect, which is three to five points lower.

For Germany, Baker et al. (1981) reported an increase in the importance of issue competence for the voting choice between 1961 and 1972. Klingemann and Taylor (1978) are more ambivalent. They note a rise in the beta effects of various domestic issues between 1961 and 1976, but a simultaneous decline in the effects of foreign policy issues; and the 1969 election seems to have been a contest between candidates (Schmidt and Strauss), almost devoid of issues.

In a number of other countries, the development since the mid-1980s is not a continuation of the trend toward rising issue voting but, rather, a halt or even reversal of that development. Of the two party systems we have used for illustration, the British elections of 1983 and 1987 seem to mark the culmination of issue dependency of the vote for the major parties; in Denmark, the 1984 election has a similar standing. In Sweden, Gilljam and Holmberg (1995, 139) present the most systematic time series encountered for issue voting in European systems. The two researchers computed the correlation (squared eta) between the party choice and an index of three issues. They selected for each of 13 elections those issues that showed the highest loading on a left-right factor. From 1956 to 1982 the eta^2 rose from 0.33 to 0.58, the general level being 0.35-0.40 during the period 1968-76, but 0.52-0.58 during 1979-91. In the recent 1994 election it dropped to 0.36.

Both in Britain and in Sweden, the reason for the particularly high level of issue voting during the mid-eighties has been put down to the emergence of new issues. These were the nuclear power and nuclear armament issues in Britain, and the nuclear power issue followed by the issue of wage earner funds in Sweden. After a solution had been found to these issues, issue voting again declined, in Britain as well as Sweden.

Linkage Studies

Most of the theories of issue voting are "bottom-up" rather than "top-down" theories. They assume or imply that issues arise among the public – although spurred or amplified by the mass media – and lead to reactions among the parties and policy-makers. Both the cognitive mobilization concept and the New Politics theory are bottom-up theories, and the rise in issue voting that they anticipate is part of a "participant voter" scenario in which the citizens are expected to play an increasing role in formulating policies. A high amount of issue voting is supposed to lead to a closer representation of the electorates's policy demands in the parliament and government.

Studies of the linkage between mass and elite indicate however that the process is much more complicated and highlight the role of the parliamentary representatives. The transmission of demands into policies depends, among other things, on the electoral rules translating votes into seats, and the roles and norms of representation which govern the attitudes and legislative behaviour of the elected representatives in parliament. The policy demands of an issue public naturally take on a particular significance if that public becomes strongly represented in the government or at least the parliament, and if its representatives feel obliged to execute the policy on which they are elected. In the theory of representation, this depends on whether they see their role as "delegates" rather than "trustees."

In the pioneering study of representation on the basis of survey evidence, Miller and Stokes (1963) compared the issue positions of U.S. Congress members with the mean positions of their constituencies and with the members' perception of that mean position. They found that on some issues, such as racial ones, the members tended to vote their constituency's position, thus acting as delegates, whereas on other issues such as foreign affairs they tended to vote their own opinion irrespective of the opinion that prevailed in their constituency, thus acting as trustees.

In political systems dominated by responsible party government, a third option would be for the member to follow his party's policy position, rather than the constituency's typical attitude, when participating in the legislative process. The question is therefore how the opinions of a party's parliamentary group interact with the opinions of the party's voters. Since the causality probably works both ways it is common to speak of "correspondence" rather than causes and effects. In terms of the model we have discussed in previous chapters we may speak of the correspondence between the party position P and the voter position V at the aggregated level of the party. However, unlike previous chapters in which we have defined P as the voter's perceptions of the party's position, we now define P as the mean position of the party's MPs. This should not invalidate earlier assumptions. The consistency model in Chapter 1 postulated that voters who are positive toward a certain party will attempt to attain consistency between V and P. This must be assumed to be valid for those who are not only positive toward a party but actually vote for it.

Likewise, MPs who want to keep their present voters should seek to attain consistency between V and P, that is, to represent the opinions of these voters. This does not mean that they can be hypothesized to mirror their voters accurately. In part they may attempt to influence their voters by taking a clearer or more ideological stance; and in part they may attempt to gain new voters by changing their stance. In fact it deserves to be mentioned that representatives are generally not representative of their voters in a statistical sense. The null hypothesis that the opinions of representatives might have come from a random sample of voters is easily re-jected. One may look at a single party and compare the mean opinion of voters on various issues against the mean opinion of MPs on the same issue. Alternatively one may look at a single issue and compare the mean opinion of the MPs with the mean opinion of their voters. Finally, one may simply compare the mean opinion of the parliament with the mean opinion of the electorate. In any case, where there are enough parlia-mentarians to examine, parliamentarians are likely to deviate significantly from public opinion. Whatever parliamentarians are, they are not delegates in the strict sense.

Rather, the pertinent questions to be researched are those dealing with the type and direction of the deviation between the two groups: how does P, the mean position of the party's representatives, deviate from V, the mean position of the party's voters for (a) different parties, (b) different issues, (c) different voter groups, and (d) different political systems? We will briefly discuss some of the leading hypotheses in the field.

First, representatives have more extreme policy positions than their voters on most issues. This shows up in a characteristic parachute-like figure of the type shown in Figure 8.1.

Figure 8.1. Typical relation between issue positions of voters and party elites

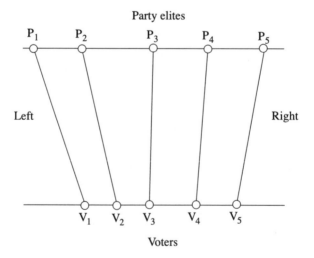

The upper line indicates the P level of representatives while the lower line indicates the V level of voters. The hypothesis implies that on the left, the representatives are more leftist than their voters, whereas on the right, the representatives are more rightist than their voters. The correspondence is greatest for center parties.

The logic of this pattern is that representatives are highly informed about the issues and need to conform to a group norm concerning the positions they take. The general public is subject to a larger amount of response error and do not have to make their issue stands public.

A different hypothesis states that representatives are to the left of their voters. This pattern was found for example in the late 1960s in France (Converse and Dupeux 1962) and Sweden (Holmberg 1974). In his comparative study of USA, Britain, Germany, and France, Dalton (1996, 242) also claims this pattern, although many of his issues deviate from it. The issue of the size of the public budget as well as the abortion issue and the nuclear energy issue display larger party-by-party deviations in P than in V. It is true, however, that the representative tend to *place* themselves to the left of their voters on the left-right scale.

Interestingly, Sweden had shifted from the left-tilting to the parachute model by 1985 (Esaiasson and Holmberg 1996, 103), as the representatives of bourgeois parties had changed their positions markedly to the right in the meantime. We may therefore suggest that the "leftist parliament" was a feature that characterized the 1960s and 1970s rather than a general feature of political representation.

A third hypothesis states that representatives are less prejudiced than their average voter. Dalton shows this for the issue of aid to third world nations, and many previous studies have showed the same for other issues that appeal to xenophobia and intolerance. On such issues representatives tend to be more liberal than their voters in each party. Thus, within the limits of such issues, the theory of the "leftist parliament" may well be true.

In respect to differences between voter groups, strong credence should be attached to the hypothesis that party identifiers show better correspondence with the representatives than non-identified voters do. This is an unambiguous consequence of the principle of consistency. Party identifiers are particularly motivated to follow the party line, and in turn party representatives are motivated to please their core voters.

The Issue Attention Cycle

Until now, linkage studies have been conducted too rarely and for too short a time to provide evidence of a rise in issue voting as a general scenario of modern political systems. Rather, these studies have opened the way toward the study of a different scenario that may be called the "transitional" scenario. This anticipates *periods* of issue voting, when particular events or problems, stemming either from domestic sources or originating outside of the country, force an issue on the government and the parties; these periods will normally be followed by periods of relative quiet. Such a scenario is consistent with what Anthony Downs (1972) calls an "issue attention cycle". According to Downs, issues first emerge among the political elite. Then they are presented to the public, causing stir and partisan changes. But as the policy proposal is carried out, a period of adaptation sets in, and in the end the policy becomes part of the political culture, the opposition against it vanishing.

Gilljam (1988), in a study of the Swedish debate over pension funds, found that Downs' model of change largely held true, except that the outcome was a watered-out compromise that nevertheless was strongly resisted by the bourgeois opposition. Thus, the new policy never became part of the political culture, and the pension funds were later dissolved by the bourgeois Bildt government.

It seems fair to judge that while Downs' model of change may characterize some types of issue, other issues tend to be voter-initiated rather than government-initiated or party-initiated. Voter-initiated issues reflect problem areas that emerge in modern societies and make good news in the media. Examples are the cultural frictions between immigrants and native populations, the failure to find employment, consumer price rises, or waves of crime. On these issues the parties seek to adapt to public opinion and represent their own voters. Party-initiated issues are those that are likely to be felt among decision-makers before they reach the population at large. Examples are membership in the European Community, problems of trade balance or public budgeting, or parliamentary tactics including threats to split a party. These cannot be seen as adaptations to public opinion; after all, the voters do not control which parties will run, nor which policies they will offer. Yet a third type of issue may be introduced by experts and media calling attention to a new phenomenon in areas such as health hazards or pollution.

Downs' idea of an issue attention cycle appears fruitful, however, even though the cycle may not be initiated by a conscious attempt by the elite to change the policy of the government. Instead, changes in public opinion may set in motion a series of adaptations with unintended consequences. In the case of Britain, a number of scholars agree that the polarization in British politics during the 1980s began with decisions made among the leaders of Labour and the Conservatives. In Denmark, the success of the Conservative-Liberal government in its first years of 1982-85 put the Social Democrats in a dilemma from which they sought to escape by polarizing foreign policy and some other policy fields, where they could count on support from the center parties. And in Germany, opposition against the Christian Democrats during the 1980s presupposed an alliance between the Social Democrats and the Greens.

Thus the issues chosen for campaign purposes in every case depended on how the party elites assessed the possibility of changing the parliamentary majority. But the autonomous role of public opinion in preparing the ground for policy proposals should not be forgotten. New issues such as crime, immigration, the environment, equal rights, and health standards have dominated the political agenda of the last two decades, much to the dismay of the governments and leading parties. Thus there seems to be no golden rule for the political process being either top-down or bottom-up that will cover all issues.

Therefore, behind the wobbles of new issues and parties making their way into the political systems of Western Europe, it is clear that something has changed decisively. In the course of the transition from the early 1970s to the late 1980s, ideologies and schemas have come to exert a stronger and more direct impact on the partisan choice than previously, often far exceeding the impact of social class or religious identity. And unlike social identities, ideologies may change so as to account for electoral change, as they are products of political discourse and exposed to sudden change. The rightward shift in Britain leading up to the 1979 election showed that ideologies may revive, whereas the fate of the Communist ideology after 1989 showed that they may almost vanish from political influence.

References

Aardal and Valen, 1989

Bernt Aardal and Henry Valen. *Velgere, partier og politisk avstand.* Oslo: Statistisk Sentralbyrå.

Achen, 1975

Christopher H. Achen. "Mass Political Attitudes and the Survey Response", *American Political Science Review*, vol. 69: 1218-31.

Adorno et al., 1950

Theodore W. Adorno, Else Frenkel-Brunswik, Daniel J. Levinson, and R. Nevitt Sandford. *The Authoritarian Personality.* New York: Norton.

Ajzen and Fishbein 1980

Icek Ajzen and Martin Fishbein. *Understanding Attitudes and Predicting Social Behavior*, Englewood Cliffs, N.J.: Prentice-Hall.

Alt, 1979

James E. Alt. *The Politics of Economic Decline.* Cambridge: Cambridge University Press.

Alt, 1984

James E. Alt. "Dealignment and the Dynamics of Partisanship in Britain", in Dalton, Flanagan, and Beck.

Anker 1992

Hans Anker. *Normal Vote Analysis.* Amsterdam: Het Spinhuiz.

Baker, Dalton and Hildebrandt, 1981

Kendall Baker, Russell Dalton, and Kai Hildebrandt. *Germany Transformed: Political Culture and the New Politics.* Cambridge, Mass.: Harvard University Press.

Berelson, Lazarsfeld and McPhee, 1954

Bernard Berelson, Paul F. Lazarsfeld and William N. McPhee, *Voting.* Chicago: Chicago University Press.

Borre, 1995

Ole Borre. "Old and New Politics in Denmark", *Scandinavian Political Studies*, vol. 18 no. 3: 187-205.

Borre, 1995a

Ole Borre. "Scope-of-Government Beliefs and Political Support", in Borre and Scarbrough, *The Scope of Government*, Chapter 12.

Borre and Goul Andersen, 1997

Ole Borre and Jørgen Goul Andersen. *Voting and Political Attitudes in Denmark*. Aarhus: Aarhus University Press.

Borre and Viegas, 1995

Ole Borre and Jose Manuel Viegas. "Government Intervention in the Economy", in Borre and Scarbrough, *The Scope of Government*, Chapter 9.

Borre and Scarbrough 1995

Ole Borre and Elinor Scarbrough (eds.). *The Scope of Government*, Oxford University Press.

Boyd 1972

Richard W. Boyd. "Popular Control of Public Policy: A Normal Vote Analysis of the 1968 Election", *American Political Science Review*, vol . 66 no. 2: 429-49.

Brody and Page 1972

Richard A. Brody and Benjamin I. Page. "Comment: The Assessment of Policy Voting", *American Political Science Review*, vol. 66: 450-58.

Brody and Page 1973

Richard Brody and Benjamin Page. "Indifference, Alienation, and Rational Decisions", *Public Choice*, 15: 1-17.

Brody and Sniderman, 1977

Richard A.Brody and Paul M. Sniderman. "From Life Space to Polling Place: the Relevance of Personal Concerns for Voting Behaviour", *British Journal of Political Science*, vol. 7: 337-60.

Brown, 1965

Roger Brown. *Social Psychology*. New York: Macmillan, and London: Collier-Macmillan.

Budge and Farlie, 1983

Ian Budge and Dennis Farlie. *Explaining and Predicting Elections*. London: Allen and Unwin.

Budge, Crewe and Farlie, 1976

Ian Budge, Ivor Crewe, and Dennis M. Farlie (eds.). *Party Identification and Beyond*. New York: Wiley.

Butler and Stokes, 1969, 1974

David Butler and Donald E. Stokes. *Political Change in Britain*. London: Macmillan.

Campbell, 1966

Angus Campbell. "A Classification of Presidential Elections" in Campbell et al.

Campbell, Converse, Miller and Stokes, 1960
Angus Campbell, Philip E. Converse, Warren E. Miller, and Donald E. Stokes. *The American Voter.* New York: Wiley.

Campbell, Converse, Miller, and Stokes, 1966
Angus Campbell, Philip E. Converse, Warren E. Miller, and Donald E. Stokes. *Elections and the Political Order.* New York: Wiley.

Carmines and Stimson, 1980
Edward G. Carmines and James A. Stimson. "The Two Faces of Issue Voting", *American Political Science Review*, vol. 74: 78-91.

Clark and Fiske 1982
Margaret Syndor Clark and Susan T. Fiske (eds.). *Affect and Cognition.* Hillesdale, New Jersey: Erlbaum.

Conover and Feldman 1984
Pamela Conover and Stanley Feldman. "How People Organize the Political World: A Schematic Model", *Journal of American Politics*, 28: 95-125.

Conover and Feldman 1986
Pamela Conover and Stanley Feldman. "Emotional Reactions to the Economy: I'm Mad as Hell and I'm Not Going to Take It Anymore", *American Journal of Political Science*, 30: 50-78.

Converse 1964
Philip E. Converse. "The Nature of Belief Systems in Mass Publics", in David Apter (ed.), *Ideology and Discontent.* New York, N.Y.: The Free Press.

Converse, 1966
Philip E. Converse. "The Concept of a Normal Vote" in Campbell et al.

Converse and Dupeux 1962
Philip E. Converse and Georges Dupeux. "Politicization of the Electorate in France and the United States", *Public Opinion Quarterly*, 26: 1-23.

Crewe and Denver 1985
Ivor Crewe and David Denver. *Electoral Change in Western Democracies.* London: Croom Helm.

Dalton, 1996
Russel J. Dalton. *Citizen Politics in Western Democracies. Public Opinion and Political Parties in the United States, Great Britain, West Germany, and France.* Chatham, N.J.: Chatham House.

Dalton, Flanagan, and Beck, 1984
Russel J. Dalton, Scott C. Flanagan, and Paul M. Beck (eds.). *Electoral Change in Advanced Industrial Democracies: Realignment or Dealignment?.* Princeton, N.J.: Princeton University Press.

Dalton and Rohrschneider, 1990
  Russel J. Dalton and Robert Rohrschneider. "Wählerwandel und Ab-
  schwächung der Parteineigung von 1972 bis 1987", in Kaase and Klingemann.

Davis and Hinich, 1966
  Otto Davis and Melvin J. Hinich. "A Mathematical Model of Policy For-
  mulation in a Democratic Society", in. J. Bernd (ed.), *Mathematical Appli-
  cations in Political Science II*. Dallas, Texas: Southern Methodist University
  Press.

Davis, Hinich and Ordeshook, 1970
  Otto Davis, Melvin J. Hinich, and Peter Ordeshook. "An Expository De-
  velopment of a Mathematical Model of the Electoral Process", *American
  Political Science Review*, vol. 64: 426-48.

Downs, 1957
  Anthony Downs. *An Economic Theory of Democracy*. New York: Harper
  and Row.

Downs, 1972
  Anthony Downs. "Up and Down with Ecology – the "Issue Attention
  Cycle", *Public Interest*, vol. 28: 38-50.

Dunleavy and Husbands, 1985
  Patrick Dunleavy and Christopher Husbands. *British Democracy at the
  Crossroads*. London: Allen and Unwin.

Easton, 1965
  David Easton. *A Systems Analysis of Political Life*. New York: Wiley and
  Sons.

Edelman 1971
  Murray Edelman. *Politics as Symbolic Action*. Chicago: Markham.

Van der Eijk and Niemöller 1983
  Cornelis van der Eijk and Broer Niemöller. *Electoral Change in the Netherlands*. Amsterdam: CT Press.

Enelow and Hinich, 1981
  James M. Enelow and Melvin J. Hinich. "A New Approach to Voter Un-
  certainty in the Downsian Spatial Model", *American Journal of Political
  Science*, vol. 25: 483-93.

Enelow and Hinich, 1982
  James M. Enelow and Melvin J. Hinich. "Ideology, Issues, and the
  Spatial Theory of Elections", *American Political Science Review*, vol. 76:
  493-501.

Enelow and Hinich 1984

James M. Enelow and Melvin J. Hinich. *The Spatial Theory of Voting: An Introduction*. New York: Cambridge University Press.

Esaiasson and Holmberg, 1996

Peter Esaiasson and Sören Holmberg. *Representation from Above*. Aldershot: Dartmouth.

Eysenck, 1954

H.J. Eysenck. *The Psychology of Politics*. London: Routledge and Kegan Paul.

Falter and Rattinger 1982

Juergen W. Falter and Hans Rattinger. "Parties, Candidates, and Issues in the German Federal Election of 1980: An Application of Normal Vote Analysis", *Electoral Studies*, vol. 1: 65-94.

Festinger, 1957

Leon Festinger. *Theory of Cognitive Dissonance*. Evanstone, Ill.: Row, Peterson.

Fiorina, 1981

Morris P. Fiorina. *Retropective Voting in American National Elections*. New Haven and London: Yale University Press.

Fishbein and Ajzen, 1975

Martin Fishbein and Icek Ajzen. *Belief, Attitude, Intention and Behaviour: An Introduction to Theory and Research*. Reading, Mass.: Addison-Wesley.

Flanagan, 1987

Scott C. Flanagan. "Values in Industrial Society", *American Political Science Review*, vol. 81: 1303-19.

Franklin 1985a

Mark Franklin. *The Decline of Class Voting in Britain: Changes in the Basis of Electoral Choice 1964-1983*, Oxford: Clarendon Press.

Franklin, 1985b

Mark Franklin. "Assessing the Rise of Issue Voting in British General Elections Since 1964", *Electoral Studies*, vol. 4: 37-56.

Franklin, Mackie and Valen

Mark Franklin, Tom Mackie, and Henry Valen (eds.). *Electoral Change*. Cambridge: Cambridge University Press, 1992.

Fuchs and Rohrschneider, 1998

Dieter Fuchs and Robert Rohrschneider. "The Electoral Process in the Unified Germany", *Studies of Democratic Government*: 93-117.

Gilljam 1988

Mikael Gilljam. *Svenska folket och löntagerfonderna*, Lund: Studentlitteratur.

Gilljam and Holmberg, 1993
Mikael Gilljam and Sören Holmberg. *Väljarna inför 90-talet.* Stockholm: Norstedts Juridik.

Gilljam and Holmberg, 1995
Mikael Gilljam and Sören Holmberg. *Väljarnas val.* Stockholm: Norstedts Juridik.

Gilljam and Oscarsson, 1996
Mikael Gilljam and Henrik Oscarsson. "Mapping the Nordic Party Space", *Scandinavian Political Studies,* vol. 19: 25-43.

Gilljam 1997
Mikael Gilljam. "The Directional Theory Under the Magnifying Glass", *Journal of Theoretical Politics,* vol. 9: 7-12.

Goldberg, 1966
Arthur M. Goldberg. "Discerning a Causal Pattern Among Data on Voting Behavior", *American Political Science Review,* vol. 60: 913-22.

Goodhart and Bhansali, 1970
C.A.E. Goodhart and R.J. Bhansali. "Political Economy", *Political Studies,* vol. 18: 43-106.

Granberg and Holmberg 1988
Donald Granberg and Soeren Holmberg. *The Political System Matters. Social Psychology and Voting Behavior in Sweden and the United States.* Cambridge: Cambridge University Press.

Heath, Jowell and Curtice, 1985
Anthony Heath, Roger Jowell, and John Curtice. *How Britain Votes.* London: Pergamon.

Heath et al., 1991
Anthony Heath et al. *Understanding Political Change: The British Voter 1964-1987.* Oxford: Pergamon.

Hibbs, 1993
Douglas A. Hibbs. *Solidarity or Egoism? The Economics of Sociotropic and Egocentric Influences on Political Behavour: Denmark in International and Theoretical Perspective.* Aarhus: Aarhus University Press.

Higgins, Hermann and Zanna, 1981
E. Tory Higgins, C. Peter Hermann and Mark P. Zanna (eds.). *Social Cognition: The Ontario Symposium.* Hillsdale, N.J.: Lawrence Erlbaum.

Hildebrandt and Dalton, 1978
Kai Hildebrandt and Russell J. Dalton. "The New Politics: Political Change or Sunshine Politics?", in Max Kaase and Klaus von Beyme (eds.), *Elections and Parties.* London/Beverly Hills: Sage.

Himmelweit et al., 1981

Hilde Himmelweit et al. *How Voters Decide*. London: Academic Press.

Himmelweit et al., 1985

Hilde Himmelweit et al. *How Voters Decide: A Model of Vote Choice Based on a Special Longitudinal Study Extending over Fifteen Years and the British Election Surveys 1970-1983*. Buckingham: Open University Press.

Hinich and Pollard, 1981

Melvin J. Hinich and Walker Pollard. "A New Approach to the Spatial Theory of Electoral Competition", *American Journal of Political Science*, vol. 25: 323-41.

Holmberg, 1974

Sören Holmberg. *"Riksdagen representerar svenska folket"*. Lund: Studentlitteratur.

Holmberg, 1981

Sören Holmberg. *Svenska väljare*. Vällingby: LiberFörlag.

Holmberg and Esaiasson, 1997

Sören Holmberg and Peter Esaiasson. *Representation from Above*. Stockholm: Norstedts Juridik.

Huseby, 1995

Beate M. Huseby. "Attitudes toward the Size of Government", in Borre and Scarbrough, *The Scope of Government*, Chapter 4.

Hyman, 1942

Herbert H. Hyman. "The Psychology of Status", *Archive of Psychology,* vol. 38.

Inglehart, 1971

Ronald Inglehart. "The Silent Revolution in Europe: Intergenerational Change in Post-Industrial Societies", *American Political Science Review*, Vol. 65: 991-1007.

Inglehart, 1977

Ronald Inglehart. *The Silent Revolution. Changing Values and Political Styles Among the Western Publics*. Princeton, N.J.: Princeton University Press.

Inglehart and Klingemann, 1974

Ronald Inglehart and Hans-Dieter Klingemann. "Party Identification, Ideological Preference and the Left-Right Dimension among Western Mass Publics", in Ian Budge, Ivor Crewe and Dennis Farlie (eds.), *Party Identification and Beyond* London: Sage.

Jenssen, 1993

Anders Todal Jenssen. *Verdival. Ny massepolitikk i Norge* [Value choice. New mass politics in Norway]. Oslo: Ad Notam Gyldendal.

Kaase, 1977

Max Kaase. *Wahlsoziologie heute. Analysen aus Anlass der Bundestagswahl 1976.* Opladen: Westdeutscher Verlag.

Kaase and Klingemann, 1983

Max Kaase and Hans-Dieter Klingemann (eds.). *Wahlen und politische System. Analysen aus Anlass der Bundestagswahl 1980.* Opladen: Westdeutscher Verlag.

Kaase and von Beyme, 1978

Max Kaase and Klaus von Beyme (eds.). *Elections and Parties. German Political Studies*, vol. 3. London/Beverly Hills: Sage.

Kaase and Klingemann, 1990

Max Kaase and Hans-Dieter Klingemann (eds.). *Wahlen und Wähler. Analysen aus Anlass der Bundestagswahl 1987.* Opladen: Westdeutscher Verlag.

Katz 1960

Daniel Katz. "The Functional Approach to the Study of Attitudes", *Public Opinion Quarterly*, 24: 163-204.

Kernell 1978

Samuel Kernell. "Explaining Presidential Popularity", *American Political Science Review*, 72: 506-22.

Kessel 1972

John H. Kessel. "Comment: The Issues in Issue Voting", *American Political Science Review*, vol. 66: 459-65.

Key, 1966

V.O. Key, Jr. *The Responsible Electorate.* New York: Vintage.

Kinder, Adams and Gronke 1989

Donald R. Kinder, George S. Adams and Paul W. Gronke. "Economics and Politics in the 1984 American Presidential Election", *American Journal of Political Science*, 33: 491-515

Kinder and Kiewiet, 1979

Donald R. Kinder and D. Roderick Kiewiet. "Economic Discontent and Political Behaviour: The Role of Personal Grievances and Collective Economic Judgments in Congressional Voting", *American Journal of Political Science*, vol. 23 no. 3: 495-527.

Klingemann and Taylor 1978

Hans-Dieter Klingemann and Charles L. Taylor. "Partisanship, Candidates and Issues: Attitudinal Components of the Vote in West German Federal Elections", in Kaase and von Beyme, pp. 97-133.

Knutsen, 1985

Oddbjørn Knutsen. *Politiske verdier, konfliktlinier og ideologi: Den norske politiske kulturen i komparativt perspektiv.* Oslo: Institutt for Statsvitenskab, Oslo Universitet.

Kramer, 1983

Gerald Kramer. "The Ecological Fallacy Revisited: Aggregate versus Individual-Level Findings on Economics and Elections", *American Political Science Review*, vol. 77: 92-111.

Krosnick and Kinder 1990

Jon A. Krosnick and Donald R. Kinder. "Altering the Foundation of Support for the President through Priming", *American Political Science Review*, vol. 84: 497-512.

Kuechler, 1990

Manfred Kuechler. "Oekologie statt Oekonomie: Waehlerpraeferenzen in Wandel?", in Kaase and Klingemann, *Wahlen und Waehler*, pp. 419-44.

Lazarsfeld, Berelson and Gaudet, 1968

Paul F. Lazarsfeld, Bernard Berelson and Hazel Gaudet. *The People's Choice*, 3rd edition, New York and London: Columbia University Press.

Lewin, 1991

Leif Lewin. *Self-Interest and Public Interest in Western Politics.* Oxford: Oxford University Press, Series on Comparative European Politics.

Lewis-Beck, 1982

Michael Lewis-Beck. "Economics and the French Voter: A Microanalysis," *Public Opinion Quarterly*, vol. 47: 347-60.

Lewis-Beck, 1988, 1990

Michael Lewis-Beck. *Economics and Elections. The Major Western Democracies.* Ann Arbor, Mich.: University of Michigan.

Lijphart, 1980

Arend Lijphart. "Language, Religion, Class and Party Choice: Belgium, Canada, Switzerland and South Africa Compared", in Richard Rose (ed.), *Electoral Participation.* Beverly Hills and London: Sage Publications.

Lipset, 1960

Seymour M. Lipset. *Political Man.* London: Heineman.

Lipset and Rokkan, 1967

Semour M. Lipset and Stein Rokkan (eds.). *Party Systems and Voter Alignments.* New York. Free Press.

Listhaug, Macdonald and Rabinowitz, 1990

Ola Listhaug, Stuart E. Macdonald, and George Rabinowitz. "A Comparative Spatial Analysis of European Party Systems", *Scandinavian Political Studies*, vol. 13: 227-54.

Listhaug, Macdonald and Rabinowitz, 1994

Ola Listhaug, Stuart E. Macdonald, and George Rabinowitz. "Ideology and Party Support in Comparative Perspective", *European Journal of Political Research*, vol. 25: 111-49.

Lomborg, 1995

Bjørn Lomborg. "Adaptive Parties in a Multiparty, Multidimensional System with Imperfect Information". Unpublished paper, Aarhus University, Department of Political Science.

Macdonald, Rabinowitz and Listhaug, 1991

Stuart E. Macdonald, Ola Listhaug, and George Rabinowitz. "Issues and Party Support in Multiparty Systems", *American Political Science Review*, vol. 85: 1107-31.

Macdonald, Rabinowitz and Listhaug, 1995

Stuart E. Macdonald, Ola Listhaug, and George Rabinowitz. "Political Sophistication and Models of Issue Voting", *British Journal of Political Science,* vol. 25: 453-83.

Maddens, 1996

Bart Maddens. "Directional Theory of Issue Voting: The Case of the 1991 Parliamentary Elections in Flanders", *Electoral Studies*, vol. 15: 53-70.

Marcus, 1988

Gregory Marcus. "The Impact of Personal and National Economic Conditions on the Presidential Vote: A Pooled Cross-Section Analysis", *American Journal of Political Science*, vol. 32: 137-54.

McAllister and Mughan, 1985

Ian McAllister and Anthony Mughan. "Attitudes, Issues, and Labour Party Decline in England, 1974-1979", *Comparative Political Studies*, vol. 18: 37-57.

McAllister and Anthony Mughan, 1987

Ian McAllister and Anthony Mughan. "Class, Attitudes, and Electoral Politics in Britain, 1974-1983", *Comparative Political Studies*, vol. 20: 47-71.

McAllister and Rose, 1984

Ian McAllister and Richard Rose. *The Nationwide Competition for Votes: The 1983 British General Election*. London: Pinter.

Meier and Campbell, 1979

Meier and Campbell. "Issue Voting: An Examination of Individually Necessary and Jointly Sufficient Conditions", *American Politics Quarterly*, vol. 7: 21-50.

Merrill, 1995

Samuel Merrill, III. "Discriminating between the Directional and Proximity Spatial Models of Electoral Competition", *Electoral Studies*, vol. 14: 273-87.

Merrill and Grofman 1997

  Samuel Merrill III and Bernhard Grofman. "Directional and Proximity Models of Voter Utility and Choice", *Journal of Theoretical Politics*, vol. 9.

Merrill and Grofman 1999

  Samuel Merrill III and Bernhard Grofman. *A Unified Theory of Vorting*. Cambridge: Cambridge University Press.

Miller, Miller, Raine and Brown 1976

  Arthur H. Miller, Warren E. Miller, Alden S. Raine, and Thad A. Brown "A Majority Party in Disarray: Policy Polarization in the 1972 Election". *American Political Science Review*, 70: 753-78.

Miller and Levitin, 1976

  Warren E. Miller and Teresa E. Levitin. *Leadership and Change: Presidential Elections from 1952 to 1976*. Cambridge, Massachusetts: Winthrop Publishers, Inc.

Miller et al., 1990

  William Miller et al. *How Voters Change: The 1987 British Election Campaign in Perspective*. Oxford: Clarendon Press.

Miller and Listhaug, 1984

  Arthur Miller and Ola Listhaug. "Economic Effects on the Vote in Norway", *Political Behavior*, vol. 4: 301-19.

Miller and Stokes, 1963

  Warren E. Miller and Donald E. Stokes. "Constituency Influence in Congress", *American Political Science Review*, vol. 57: 45-56.

Morris and Rabinowitz 1997

  Irwin L. Morris and George Rabinowitz. "On the Coexistence of Directional and Proximity Voters", *Journal of Theoretical Politics*, vol. 9.

Müller-Rommel, 1990

  Ferdinand Müller-Rommel. "New Political Movements and 'New Politics' Parties in Western Europe", in Russel J. Dalton and Manfred Kuechler (eds.), *Challenging the Political Order. New Social and Political Movements in Western Democracies*. Cambridge: Polity Press.

Nannestad, 1989

  Peter Nannestad. *Reactive Voting in Danish General Elections 1971-79: A Revisionist Interpretation*. Aarhus: Aarhus University Press.

Nannestad and Paldam, 1994

  Peter Nannestad and Martin Paldam. "The VP Function: A Survey of the Literature on Vote and Popularity Functions after 25 Years", *Public Choice*, vol. 79: 213-45.

Nannestad and Paldam, 1995

Peter Nannestad and Martin Paldam. "It's the Government's Fault", *European Journal of Political Research*, vol. 28: 33-62.

Nannestad and Paldam, 1997

Peter Nannestad and Martin Paldam. "From the Pocketbook of Welfare Man: A Pooled Cross-Section Study of Economic Voting in Denmark, 1986-92", *British Journal of Political Science*, vol. 27: 119-36.

Newcomb, 1943.

Theodore M. Newcomb. *Personality and Social Change: Attitude Formation in a Student Community*. New York: Dryden.

Nie with Andersen, 1974.

Norman H. Nie with Kristi Andersen. "Mass Belief Systems Revisited: Political Change and Attitude Structure", *Journal of Politics*, vol. 36: 540-87.

Norris, 1997

Pippa Norris. *Electoral Change in Britain Since 1945*. Oxford: Blackwell.

Page 1977

Benjamin I. Page. "Elections and Social Choice: The State of the Evidence", *American Journal of Political Science*, 21: 639-68.

Petrocik, 1996

John R. Petrocik. "Issue Ownership in Presidential Elections, with a 1980 Case Study", *American Journal of Political Science*, vol. 40: 825-50.

Pettersen, 1995

Per Arnt Pettersen. "The Welfare State: The Security Dimension", in Borre and Scarbrough.

Pierce 1997

Roy Pierce. "Directional Versus Proximity Models", *Journal of Theoretical Politics*, vol. 9.

Pomper, 1972

Gerald Pomper. "From Confusion to Clarity: Issues and American Voters, 1956-1968", *American Political Science Review*, vol. 66: 415-28.

Rabinowitz and Macdonald, 1989

George Rabinowitz and Stuart E. Macdonald. "A Directional Theory of Issue Voting", *American Political Science Review*, vol. 83: 93-121.

Rabinowitz, Macdonald and Listhaug, 1991

George Rabinowitz, Stuart E. Macdonald, and Ola Listhaug. "New Players in an Old Game: Party Strategy in Multiparty Systems", *Comparative Political Studies*, vol. 24: 147-85.

RePass 1971

David E. RePass. "Issue Salience and Party Choice", *American Political Science Review*, 65: 389-400.

Rivers, 1988

Douglas Rivers. "Heterogeneteity in Models of Electoral Change", *American Journal of Political Science*, vol. 32: 737-57.

Rohrschneider 1993

Robert Rohrschneider, "New Left Versus Old Party Realignments. Environmental Attitudes, Party Politics, and Partisan Affiliations in Four West European Countries", *Journal of Politics*, vol. 55: 682-701.

Rohrschneider and Fuchs 1998

Robert Rohrschneider and Dieter Fuchs. "A New Electorate? The Economic Trends and Electoral Choice in the 1994 Federal Election", *Studies of Democratic Government*, pp. 67-91.

Rokeach 1973

Milton Rokeach. *The Nature of Human Values*. New York: Free Press, and London: Collier Macmillan.

Roller 1995

Edeltraud Roller. "Political Agendas and Beliefs about the Scope of Government", in Borre and Scarbrough, *The Scope of Government*, Chapter 3.

Rose and McAllister, 1986

Richard Rose and Ian McAllister. *Voters Begin to Choose*. London: Sage.

Rose and McAllister, 1990

Richard Rose and Ian McAllister. *The Loyalities of Voters*. London: Sage.

Rusk and Borre, 1974

Jerrold M. Rusk and Ole Borre. "The Changing Party Space in Danish Voter Perceptions, 1971-73", in Ian Budge, Ivor Crewe, and Dennis Farlie (eds.), *Party Identifications and Beyond*.

Rusk and Borre, 1976

Jerrold M. Rusk and Ole Borre. "The Changing Party Space in Danish Voter Perceptions, 1971-73", *European Journal of Political Science*, vol. 2: 329-61.

Särlvik and Crewe, 1983

Bo Särlvik and Ivor Crewe. *Decade of Dealignment: The Conservative Victory of 1979 and Electoral Trends in the 1970s*. Cambridge: Cambridge University Press.

Sears, Hensler and Speer, 1979

David O. Sears, Carl P. Hensler, and Leslie K. Speer. "White's Oppositon to 'Busing': Self-Interest or Symbolic Politics?", *American Political Science Review*, vol. 73: 369-84.

Sears, Lau, Tyler and Allen 1980
David O. Sears, Richard R. Lau, Tom R. Tyler, and Harris M. Allen, Jr. "Self-Interest vs. Symbolic Politics in Political Attitudes and President-ial Vote", *American Political Science Review*, 74: 670-84.

Sears and Citrin 1982
David O. Sears and Jack Citrin. *Tax Revolt: Something for Nothing in California.* Cambridge, Mass.: Harvard University Press.

Stokes 1963
Donald E. Stokes. "Spatial Models of Party Competition", *American Political Science Review*, vol. 57: 368-77.

Stouffer 1955
Samuel A. Stouffer. *Communism, Conformity, and Civil Liberties.* New York: Doubleday.

Studies of Democratic Government, 1998
Studies of Democratic Government – A Collection, Social Science Research Center (WZB), Berlin

Studlar and Welch, 1981
D.T. Studlar and S. Welch. "Mass Attitudes and Political Issues in Britain", *Comparative Political Studies*, vol. 14: 327-56.

Taylor and Crocker, 1981
Shelley E. Taylor and Jennifer Crocker. "Schematic Bases of Social Information Processing", in Higgins, Hermann and Zanna.

Triandis and Davis 1965
Harry C. Triandis and E.E. Davis. "Race and Belief as Determinants of Behavioral Intentions", *Journal of Personality and Social Psychology*, 2: 715-25.

Valen 1981
Henry Valen. *Valg og politikk.* Oslo: NKS-Forlaget.

Van der Eijk and Niemöller, 1983
C. van der Eijk and B. Niemöller. *Electoral change in the Netherlands.* Amsterdam: CT-press.

Van Deth and Scarbrough, 1995
Jan van Deth and Elinor Scarbrough (eds.). *The Impact of Values.* Oxford: Oxford University Press.

Westholm 1997
Anders Westholm. "Distance versus Direction: The Illusory Defeat of the Proximity Theory of Electoral Choice", *American Political Science Review*, 91: 865-83.

Zajonc 1980
Robert Zajonc. "Feeling and Thinking: Preferences Need No Inferences", *American Psychologist*, 35: 151-75.

Subject index

Abortion issue 93, 95-96, 107, 133, 139
Additive index -30, 53, 80, 87
Advertisement -106
Affect, affective judgments 20, 66, 73, 81-82, 129-30, 132
Age -24, 127
Agenda, political 13, 15, 17, 89-91, 99-101, 105-07, 109, 141
Agenda-setting studies v102
Agrarian parties 9
Aid to developing or poorer countries 91, 94-97, 139
Alliance vote, British 59
Anti-immigration parties 90, 93, 106, 133-34
Attitude measurement 10, 128
Authoritarian issues 88, 95

Belief systems 11, 41, 83, 101
Bildt, Carl 140
Boer War 9
Bonds, psychological 14-15,
Bourgeois parties 64, 88, 119
Bourgeoisie 53-54, 87, 88, 95, 116-18, 134, 139-40
Britain 92, 123, 136, 139
Budget items 92, 139-40

Campaign 41, 59, 61, 100, 106, 109, 119-21, 124, 131, 141
Campaign communication or debate 99, 108
Campaign platform 81
Campus unrest 93
Canada 108
Candidate orientation or evaluation 10, 110
Capitalism 12
Capitalist parties 89
Carter, Jimmy 120, 121
Catch-all parties 128
Causality, causal process 20, 24, 34, 39-42, 66, 80, 82, 123, 137

CDU/CSU party, government or vote (Germany) 12, 47, 93, 141
Center parties 70, 78, 82, 139, 141
Church-goers 85, 128
City-block distance 67
Civil order issues 108
Class identification 25-29
Class interest 88
Class position 11, 24-26, 41
Class voting 24, 27-28, 135
Clustering of issues 28, 46-47, 83, 92
Cognition, cognitive judgments 127, 129-30
Cognitive consistency 14, 19, 79, 130
Cognitive mobilization 131-32, 136
Collinearity problem 30
Columbia scholars 100
Communications research 10, 102
Communist parties or ideology 89, 141
Competence of governments or leaders 16, 61, 120, 126, 135
Consensus issue 64, 99, 100
Conservative parties 9, 100, 107-08, 120, 131
Conservative Party (Denmark) 71, 141
Conservative Party or vote (British) 12, 22-27, 29-32, 34, 37, 48-51, 55, 59, 60-70, 76, 80-82, 97-98, 103, 105, 124-25, 135
Consumer theory or model 58-59, 65, 66
Controls for social position or class 24-27, 37, 135
Controls for other issues 29, 37, 41
Controls for party identification 37, 43, 46-47, 49, 57, 63, 115, 117
Controls for past vote 53, 110
Controls for left-right position 47, 88, 123
Controls for utility differences 77
Credibility of governments 16, 18, 114
Crime issue 64, 94-95, 120, 124, 133, 140, 141

Critical election 56
Culture and arts, spending on 92

Danish People's Party 32
Dealignment 24, 26, 49
Death penalty 135
Defence issue 62, 91-92
Democrats 42, 115, 120
Democratic liberties 89
Democratic norms 90
Democratic vote or party (USA) 43-46, 64, 93, 113, 121
Denmark 21, 136, 141
Deviating elections 56, 134
Directional theory 12, 20, 73-79, 81-82, 130
Distortion of party position 15, 30, 50, 80-81
Domestic policies 111, 115, 135
Don't know responses 21
Dreyfus affair 9
Dutch studies 12

East Germany 133
Easy issues 132
Economic equality 94
Economic growth issue 16, 61, 102, 122, 128
Economic issues 12, 86-87, 91, 95, 98, 133-34
Economic problems 116-18
Economic restraint 117
Economic security 91
Economic voting 12, 122-23, 128
Education, issue of 92, 124
Education, length of 131
Education, level of 30, 90, 94, 132-34
Education, spending on 31
Ego-defensive function 130
Elite behaviour 59, 136, 140-41
Elmira study 100
Employment 128, 140
Environment 90, 99, 106, 124, 141
Environmental protection 84, 91-94, 102, 105, 107, 133
Equal treatment or opportunities 90, 95-97, 141
Erie County study 10
Ethnic issues 83
Ethnicity 11

Ethnocentrism 95
EU or European Union 16, 21, 140
Euclidean distance 67
Eurobarometer 87, 122
European Common Market or Community 21

Factor analysis 91, 130
Farm problems 120
Fascist parties 89
FDP party (Germany) 47
Follow-up questions 101, 103
Ford, Gerald 113
Foreign countries, relations with 111, 122, 137
Foreign policy 115, 121, 135, 141
Former vote 53-56, 110
Framing of issues 121
France 9, 123, 139
Functional theory in sociology 100
Functional theory of attitudes 130
Funnel of causality 42

Gallup Poll 102
Game theory 63
Gender 46
Generations 11, 46, 57, 83, 89
Geographical region 11
Germany 12, 47, 93, 123, 133, 135, 139, 141
Government 118
Green dimension 95
Green parties 90, 106, 133-34
Green party (Germany) 141

Handling of issues or problems 114, 118-21
Hard issues 132
Health issues 62, 95
Health services, spending on 31, 92, 96
Health standards 124-25, 141
Homosexuals, rights of 135
Hostages (in Teheran) 121
Humphrey, Hubert 115-16

Immigration issue or policy 16, 94, 104, 106, 133, 140-41
Importance of issues 16-17, 25, 40, 61, 63, 66, 75, 89, 91-92, 99-109, 114, 121, 129, 133, 135

Income distribution 13, 83
Income redistribution issue 13, 22-26, 31, 34, 35, 38, 87, 95, 97, 125
Income, voter's 24, 127
Indifferent voters 13
Industrial growth issue 105
Inflation issue 16, 61, 62, 79, 102, 105, 118, 120, 122
Information, level of 30-31 131
Ingroup/outgroup schema 132
Intellectuals 88
Interest, political 30-32, 131-32
Intolerance 139
Iran, Iran-Contra scandal 120-21
Ireland 108
Irrational reactions or voters 15, 50, 129
Isolationism 121
Issue attention 140-41
Issue ownership 119-21
Issue publics 101-02, 107, 121, 137
Issue space 29, 61, 92-93
Italy 123, 134

Johnson, Lyndon 114

Kinnock, Nei l 124
Knowledge function 130

Labour Party or vote (British) 12, 22-24, 30, 34-35, 50, 55, 59-70, 76, 79, 103, 105, 124, 135, 141
Language issues 83
Law and order issue 62, 88, 91, 95, 109
Law enforcement, spending on 92
Learning, theory of 112
Left-right attitudes 38
Left-right issues or values 24, 84, 92, 133
Left-right scale or axis, dimension 59-60, 64, 83, 88, 90, 94, 123, 136, 139
Left-right schema 84, 90, 132
Left-right self-placement 47, 49, 85-87
Left-wing vote or parties 95
Legislative roll calls 59, 85
Liberal Democratic Party or vote (British) 22-23, 60-61, 64-65, 67-70, 76-77
Liberal parties 9, 100
Liberal Party (Denmark) 60

Living standards 124-25
Log linear models 21
Logic of issue voting 9, 100, 106, 114
Logic 5, 63, 75, 82, 125, 139
Logistic regression, log ods 33, 37, 49, 117

Maintaining elections 56
Major, John 124
Marginal utility 133
Marihuana 93
Marxist theory 88
Measurement error 52
Median voter 64
Mediated issue positions 62, 115, 126
Michigan school or model 10-11, 41-43, 56, 61, 65, 83, 101-02, 110
Middle class 26-28, 90
Minority rights 88, 90
Moral or moral-religious issues 83, 90, 91, 93, 108
MPs, positions of 137-39

National self-determination 16
Nationalization issue 28-29, 36, 38, 48-49, 51, 62, 64, 87, 95-97, 103, 125, 135
Nearest party 17, 58-62, 112, 129
Netherlands 12, 55
New Politics dimension or cleavage 83, 90, 92-95, 135
New politics issues 90, 93-95, 97-98, 133
New Politics paradigm or theory 84, 90-92, 95-96, 98, 132-34, 136
Newspaper 102, 106
Nixon, Richard 111, 113
Nonlinearity, problem of 21, 32
Nonlinearity model 33, 37
Non-rational behaviour 80, 130
Non-salient issues 102-03
Normal vote 43-47, 56, 101
Northern Ireland issue 96-97
Norway 12, 74-75, 91, 93, 133
Norwegian studies or researchers 13, 91
Nuclear armament issue 28-29
Nuclear defence 95, 135
Nuclear power issue 93, 95, 133, 139
Nuffield College 5

Occupation 127-28, 132
Oil crisis of 1979 121
Old age pensions 92, 129
Old politics dimension or cleavage 90-91, 94-98, 133
Open-ended responses 101
Opinion change 34-35, 38, 40-41, 50, 64
Oxford Dictionary 13

Panel analysis 40-41, 50, 53, 57
Panel data 50, 55, 113
Panel studies 40, 51, 53
Panic, waves of 131-32
Party competition 85, 135
Party identification 10, 37, 41-50, 55-57, 66, 80, 82, 87, 102, 113, 115-17, 122, 126, 133
Party images 109, 131
Party loyalty 10, 40, 41, 50, 56, 115, 117, 134
Party programs 17, 59, 64, 106
Party strategy 63, 74, 80, 106, 117, 119, 127
Party switching 51, 53-55
Party sympathy 13, 55, 67, 80, 85, 88
Peace issue 18, 99
Penalty, penalty zone (in directional model) 75, 82
Pension fund issue (in Sweden) 140
Perceived distance or position 79-81
Performance of governments 13, 15-18, 61-62, 99-100, 109, 112-15, 117-22, 124, 126
Permissiveness 95
Personal finances or income 111, 122, 130
Petty bourgeoisie 88
Physical security 91
Pocket-book voting 13, 128, 130
Policy image 62-63
Policy space 93
Political discourse 84, 141
Political movements 85, 88
Political interest 30-32, 131
Pollution 109, 140
Pornography 95
Postindustrial society 90, 132-34
Postindustrial theory 132-33
Postmaterial values 89, 92, 98, 133

Postwar generation 12
Poverty 96-97
Pragmatic function 130
Priming of issues 107, 121
Price 125, 140
Price stability 128
Priority of issues 99-02, 109
Private business 13, 28, 87
Privatization issue 28-29, 36-37, 48-49, 96-97, 103, 125, 135
Probit analysis 111
Professional organizations 133
Progressive Party (Denmark) 32, 71-72, 77
Progressive taxation 13
Property ownership 88
Protecting the countryside 95
Proximity theory or model 12, 20, 61-63, 65-68, 70, 72-79, 82, 100, 102, 105, 112-13, 115, 129-130
Public budgeting 140

Quality-of-life issues 90

Racial characteristics 127
Racial equality 89, 93
Racial attitudes 96, 128-29
Racial segregation issue 132, 137
Radical Liberal party (Denmark) 71, 75
Random answer 24, 30, 41, 51
Random decision 78
Rationality of voters 58, 88, 128-29
Reagan, Ronald 120-21
Realigning elections 56- 57
Recall data 53, 55-56
Redistribution issues 34-35, 96, 102, 108, 125
Reference groups 42, 46, 85
Refugee issue 32, 37-38, 95, 104
Regulation of business 10, 48, 71
Relational values 133
Reliability of responses 30, 40-41, 51-52, 133
Religion 11
Religious voters 91, 127, 131, 141
Religious issues 83, 91, 93, 108
Religious parties 128
Religious values 89, 93
Republican party (German) 93

Republican vote or party (USA) 43-45, 64, 93, 115, 120-21
Response error 41, 51-52, 56, 139
Retrospective voting 11, 18, 109, 111-14, 122
Reverse causality 42
Reward and punishment theory 64, 110
Rightwing vote or parties 32, 38, 104
Roosevelt, F.D. 10

Sampling 11
Scandinavia 88
Schema theory 82, 84-85, 87, 90-91, 93, 132, 141
Schmidt, Helmut 136
School leaving age 31
School-busing issue 128
Self-interest 12, 88, 127-30, 132-33
Self-reliability 130
Sex 24
Sexual minorities 93
Short-term forces 43, 55-56, 134
Social benefits, services or welfare 31, 62
Social class 24-27, 29, 40-41, 43, 46, 55, 90, 94, 128, 135, 141
Social Democratic party (Denmark) 60, 64, 71, 75, 77, 94, 117-19, 141
Social equality or inequality 118
Social position 20, 24-25, 127
Social reforms 53, 87, 94, 107
Social security 120
Social service 83, 96, 117
Social welfare 95, 116
Socialist 87, 100, 120
Socialist parties 9, 89, 128
Socialist People's party (Denmark) 71
Sociotropic voting 13, 122-26, 128
Spain 123
Spatial model, theory or approach 13, 20, 58-59, 61, 63, 65, 99, 101, 132
SPD party, government or vote (Germany) 12, 47, 141
State control or regulation of business 87, 94
Strauss, Franz Josef 136
Sweden 12, 75, 92-93, 101, 136, 139
Swedish studies or researchers 13, 101, 140

Symbolic action or politics 127-28, 130-32
Symbolic function 130

Tax issue or level 31, 91, 96, 102, 109, 116, 120, 125
Thatcher, Margaret 37
Third term in office 41
Trade balance 140
Trade union membership 10, 127
Trade-off items 102, 105-06
True position or distance 79-80
TV time 106

Unemployment benefits 92
Unemployment issue 61-62, 79, 90, 102, 105, 120, 122, 124-25
United States 74, 139
Unreliability 40-41, 51-52
Urban riots 93
Utility 13, 22, 58, 59, 61, 65-67, 70, 73-80, 82, 133

Valence issues 61, 99-102, 105-07, 109, 111, 113-15, 118
Value change 89-91, 96, 134
Value dimensions 88-89, 91
Value space 93
Values 12, 18, 89-93, 96, 100, 133
Vietnam issue 44-45, 113, 132
Violent crime, issue of 94

Wage increases, issue of 94, 136
Wallace, George 45-46
World War 10-11, 89
War, risk or threats of 111, 115, 118, 124
Watergate scandal 113
Weber, Max 88
Welfare benefits or services 13, 91, 96-97, 102
Will of the people 10
Women's rights 91
Working class, workers 26-28, 85, 88

Xenophobia, xenophobic attitudes 37, 139

Zone of responsibility 75, 82

Author Index

Aardal, Bernt 91
Achen, Christopher H. 47
Adorno, Theodore 88
Allen, Harris M., Jr. 128
Andersen, Kristi 52, 83

Baker, Kendall 83, 89
Beck, Paul M. 49, 131
Berelson, Bernard 10, 41, 100
Bhansali, R.J. 122
Borre, Ole 87, 90, 92, 94, 135
Boyd, Richard W. 11, 44-45
Brody, Richard A. 11, 46, 130
Brown, Roger 13
Budge, Ian 11, 47, 107-08
Butler, David 11, 48, 61, 86

Campbell, Angus 10, 13, 41-42, 56, 57
Carmines, Edward G. 132
Gaudet 10, 41
Conover, Pamela 84, 129
Converse, Philip E. 10-11, 41, 43, 51, 83, 101, 139
Crewe, Ivor 11, 24, 47, 62
Crocker, Jennifer 84
Curtice, John 28, 59, 62, 79

Dalton, Russell 18, 49, 83, 90, 93, 131, 133, 139
Deth, Jan van 89
Downs, Anthony 11, 58, 61, 65, 140
Dunleavy, Patrick 30, 62
Dupeux, Georges 139

Edelman, Murray 128
Eijk, Cornelis van der 55
Esaiasson, Peter 139
Eysenck, H.J. 88

Falter, Juergen W. 47
Farlie, Dennis M. 11, 47, 107-08
Feldman, Stanley 84, 129
Fiorina, Morris P. 111-14

Franklin, Mark 28, 48, 131, 135
Flanagan, Scott C. 49, 90, 131
Fuchs, Dieter 133

Gilljam, Mikael 88, 91, 135, 140
Goodhart, C.A.E. 122
Goul Andersen, Jørgen 87, 90, 94
Granberg, Donald 50, 52
Grofman, Bernard 74

Heath, Anthony 28, 59, 62, 79, 95, 135
Hensler, Carl P. 128
Hibbs, Douglas A. 122
Hildebrandt, Kai 83, 90, 93
Himmelweit, Hilde 55, 65
Holmberg, Sören 50, 51, 91, 93, 135, 139
Husbands, Christopher 30, 62
Huseby, Beate M. 92
Hyman, Herbert H. 42

Inglehart, Ronald 11, 85, 89, 96, 131, 133

Jenssen, Anders Todal 90-91, 133
Jowell, Roger 28, 59, 62, 79

Katz, Daniel 130
Kessel, John H. 46
Key, V.O. 11, 110-12, 114
Kiewiet, D. Roderick 12, 122-23, 128
Kinder, Donald R. 12, 121-23, 128
Klingemann, Hans-Dieter 85, 135
Knutsen, Oddbjørn 90-91
Kramer, Gerald 122
Krosnik, Jon A. 121
Kuechler, Manfred 133

Lazarsfeld, Paul F. 10, 41, 100
Lau, Richard R. 128
Levitin, Teresa E. 93
Lewin, Leif 122
Lewis-Beck, Michael 122-23

Lijphart, Arend 83
Lipset, Seymour M. 11, 88, 91
Listhaug, Ola 74, 75, 80

Macdonald, Stuart E. 12, 73-75, 80
Maddens, Bart 74
McAllister, Ian 95, 96
McPhee, William N. 100
Meier 41
Merrill, Samuel III 74, 79
Miller, Warren E., 10, 93, 135
Mughan, Anthony 95-96
Müller-Rommel, Ferdinand 90

Nannestad, Peter 85, 122
Newcomb, Theodore M. 42
Nie, Norman H. 52, 83
Niemöller, Broer 55
Norris, Pippa 37, 135

Oscarsson, Henrik 88

Page, Benjamin I. 11, 46
Paldam, Martin 122
Pettersen, Per Arnt 37
Petrocik, John R. 119-21
Pomper, Gerald M. 11, 52

Rabinowitz, George 12, 73-75, 80
Rattinger, Hans 47
RePass, David E. 102-03
Rivers, Douglas M. 102
Rohrschneider, Robert 133
Rokeach, Milton 89, 96
Rokkan, Stein 11, 91
Roller, Edeltraud 91

Särlvik, Bo 24
Scarbrough, Elinor 89
Sears, David O. 128
Sniderman, Paul M. 130
Speer, Leslie K. 128
Stimson, James A. 132
Stokes, Donald E. 10-11, 48, 61, 86, 99, 101, 135

Taylor, Charles L. 84, 135
Taylor, Shelley E. 84
Tyler, Tom R. 128

Valen, Henry 91, 93

Westholm, Anders 76

Zajonc, Robert 129